Life Around Morecambe Bay

by Cedric Robinson (Guide to the Kent Sands)
and W.R. Mitchell (Editor of "Cumbria")

CEDRIC ROBINSON LEADING A PARTY TOWARDS THE KENT

Dalesman Books
1986

The Dalesman Publishing Company Ltd.,
Clapham, via Lancaster, LA2 8EB
First published 1986
© Cedric Robinson & W.R. Mitchell, 1986
ISBN: 0 85206 865 4
Printed by Fretwell & Cox Ltd.,
Goulbourne Street, Keighley, West Yorkshire

WALKERS MUSTER AT JENNY BROWN'S POINT BEFORE CROSSING THE SANDS TO GRANGE

THE CARRIAGE CROSSING, 1985

Contents

Illustrations

Cover pictures by courtesy of Peter Cherry.
Drawings by Olive Robinson.
Holker Hall: 48, 49, 50, 51. *W.R. Mitchell:* 1, 8, 11, 17, 19 (right), 23, 27, 39, 53, 57, 59, 60, 63, 64, 65. *D. Buckley:* 2. *K.G. Ettridge:* 3, 29. *Morecambe Visitor:* 5. *Westmorland Gazette:* 60. *Yorkshire Television:* 8, 44, 45. *Lancaster Maritime Museum:* 12, 154, 20 (top), 20 (bottom right). *Collection of J. Dodgson:* 34 (top right), 41. *N. Wolstenholme:* 13 (top), 41. *Collection of Jim Braid:* 14, 18, 19 (left). *T. Parker:* 16. *W.S. Garth:* 20 (bottom left). *Telegraph and Argus:* 22. *R.H. Humber:* 24 (left). *J. Hardman:* 24 (right). *West Cumberland Advertiser:* 31, 66. *Collection of Peter Wain:* 34 (top left), 34 (bottom). *Paul Nickson:* 40. *Lancashire Evening Post:* 42. *Ethel Tyson:* 47. *Tyne-Tees Television:* 67. *Evening Gazette, Blackpool:* 32. *Jean Jackson:* 70 (left). *Leslie Stringer:* 70 (right).

JIM BRAID AND HIS SON, DAVID, AT THE MOUTH OF THE LUNE

Foreword by
H.R.H. The Duke of Edinburgh

(portrayed herewith during a historic
Sands crossing in May, 1985)

BUCKINGHAM PALACE.

    I had seen Morecambe Bay from the air any number of times but it was only when I came to take part in the Horse Driving Trials at Holker in 1975 that I was able to see the full beauty of the sands in their setting of lakeland hills, and to experience the very special atmosphere of that unique piece of countryside. I got to know the sands even more intimately when I took part in the historic crossing of the Kent estuary by horse-drawn carriages to mark the tenth anniversary of the Trials.

    Cedric Robinson, the holder of the ancient office of "Queen's Guide", sat beside me as he guided the party safely across the sands from Silverdale to Grange-over-Sands and I was intrigued to hear his many stories about the sands and the influence they have exerted on the social and economic life of the local people.

    Today the sands no longer provide a short cut for Stage-coaches between Lancaster and Ulverston, but they remain just as valuable for their beauty and for the wildlife which they support. Such sensitive natural areas are most at risk when traditional uses have declined and when no thought has been given to their future.

    I hope that this book will help to preserve the local history of the Morecambe Bay sands and to draw attention to the need to care for the whole Bay as a sanctuary for wildlife as well as a beautiful recreational area for future generations to enjoy.

1986

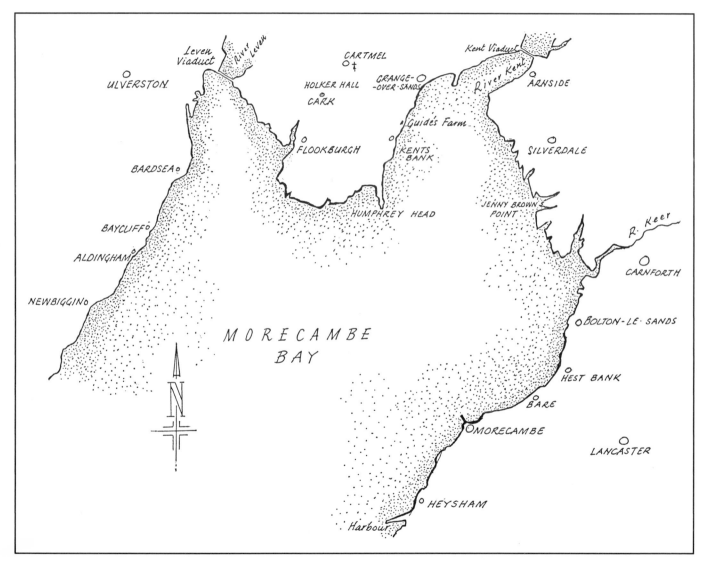

ULVERSTON

Leven Viaduct

River Leven

CARTMEL

Kent Viaduct

HOLKER HALL

CARK

GRANGE-OVER-SANDS

River Kent

ARNSIDE

Guide's Farm

FLOOKBURGH

KENTS BANK

SILVERDALE

BARDSEA

HUMPHREY HEAD

JENNY BROWN'S POINT

R. Keer

BAYCUFF

CARNFORTH

ALDINGHAM

MORECAMBE BAY

BOLTON-LE-SANDS

NEWBIGGIN

HEST BANK

N

BARE

MORECAMBE

LANCASTER

HEYSHAM

Harbour

MAP DRAWN BY EDWARD GOWER

Across the Bay

BROWN SHORE CRAB

YOU DO NOT really know Morecambe Bay until you have walked across it, following the long walk, from Hest Bank to Kents Bank: eight miles of pounding the finely ribbed sand and sloshing through two lively watercourses, Keer and Kent, that drain a considerable part of the Lake District. Even then, you have only crossed the Kent Sands, a corner of the Bay, which in total area covers about 200 square miles. Broad but comparatively shallow, Morecambe Bay is awesome. When the tide has ebbed, falling back for a maximum distance of up to nine miles, there remains a wilderness of sand and sun-flecked water. A television producer with a romantic disposition called it The Wet Sahara.

A flow tide crosses the Bay with the speed of a good horse. There are few truly level areas. The Bay undulates gently. So the tide surges up the gutters, it performs pincer movements around the wharfs (banks) and it bubbles and boils against the mussel-encrusted skeers, the home of conger eels, some of which weigh anything up to 60 pounds and are well over six feet in length. In due course, the incoming tide spreads itself over thousands of acres of inter-tidal marsh and smacks its lips against firm land.

On the maps are marked the channels of rivers that eventually pour their waters into the Lune Deeps. Those channels are ever-changing. (The maps are never quite up-to-date!). A spectacular storm in 1977 inflicted extensive damage to the coastline and, overnight, shifted the course of the mighty Kent from one side of the Bay to the other. A Morecambe fisherman says: "A mile below Heysham Harbour, the water was once 11 fathoms deep. It's now much shallower. Why, when I was a lad, boats sailed from the T-end of Morecambe's Central Pier." The Bay has silted up at an impressive speed, the process accelerating when the railway was built beside the sea. The tide used to lap against what is now the main street at Grange. It flowed round the mound on which Ravenstown now stands — a mound which is now well back from the sea. At Flookburgh, the fishermen seek shrimps and flukes with nets that are borne along a mile of marsh road on tractor-drawn trailers.

The fishermen of Morecambe, using their locally built trawlers — which were originally under sail, and have the fine lines of yachts — were aware that even in the calmest weather a strong tidal current running over the skeers could make the sea bubble and boil. (In 1946, from Raap Skeer, a Morecambe trawl collected a conger eel that was six foot two and a-half inches in length and weighed something over 50 pounds before it was gutted. It would have been quite capable of biting the flesh from a man's hand with its terrible teeth!).

A Flookburgh fisherman picks his way across the gentle undulations and the channels of low-tide Morecambe Bay with the confidence of a city man using some well-known streets. Dick Proctor, who lives at a house near the shore at Silverdale, is one of those who knows the Bay in fine detail. He has seen innumerable subtle changes, such as the re-appearance of a skeer that had been covered by sand for over 80 years. What the tide gives, the tide can take away. Fisherfolk talk about "melgraves", deep holes scoured by the incoming tide and then filled with a sloppy sand at the ebb. A quicksand results and it can vary from a few inches to a depth sufficient to swallow up a man. Cedric needs for his job as Sands Guide an awesome knowledge of the Bay, its appearance and tidal quirks. "Sometimes a heavy downpour of rain can help you to cross a river by causing the water to spread, though it can also have the opposite effect at times, concentrating the river into one area — we call it a gullet — where it can be very deep and dangerous."

Morecambe Bay looks desolate to anyone who beholds it from the shore, but the whole area throbs with life. The Sands are a rich source of food for birds. The oyster-catcher, or sea pie, a common local bird, uses its red neb to penetrate and twist open a cockle or mussel. In summer, there is a swirl of bird life, gulls and terns, over Walney and Foulney, with the terns collecting small fish that gleam with the brightness of silver as they catch the sunlight while being borne to the nestlings. Eiders by the hundred dine on mussels. Shelduck use their special beaks to sieve food from the mud and they nest in old rabbit burrows. In autumn, myriad birds from the northlands — ducks, geese, waders — infuse life into the Bay.

Dr. F. W. Hogarth, of Morecambe, believed that the curious duplication of the vowel sound in local names denotes their Norse origin. Words still used by the Morecambe Bay fisherman have this characteristic. There is *skeer,* already mentioned. This patch of rough sea bed will ebb dry or is very shallow at low water, forming a *roost,*

Above: **A "brob", composed of pieces of laurel and used to mark a route at the approaches to the Kent.**

Below: **When Argo Ashton organised walks from Hest Bank 20 years ago, he carried a flag.**

which is the tidal-rip or drop-off, and the most dangerous of all spots in a gale. *Craam* is a name for the iron rake with a long wooden shaft that is used for raking up bunches of mussels or cockles, and *laaster* is the three-pronged fishing spear used to impale fish in shallow water (and employed down the years by river poachers after salmon!). *Haaf,* said to be the old Norse word for sea, gave its name for the largest hand-net, which is used to take salmon and sea trout, a method more ancient than effective!

Grave Norsemen, and graver monks, knew Morecambe Bay. The latter scurried across the Bay at low tide, intent on business connected with their Orders. The religious house appointed the first Guides for the Sands and at the chantry chapels established at the ends of the most commonly used crossings, prayers were said for safe passages. One chantry stood on Chapel Island, a speck of land at the mouth of the Leven estuary. Coaches, people, droves of cattle and sheep — all used the low-tide crossing. Before turnpike roads were established, a fleet of coaches offered passengers quick if uneasy transport from just north of Lancaster into Furness.

The Sands route was used because it sliced miles off the landward journey and was free from dust, which in summer almost suffocated travellers on the unmetalled, cross country roads. The Sands traffic quickly declined with the opening of the railway locally in 1857. (Carriages were absent from the Kent crossing until 1985 when the Duke of Edinburgh led a group of horse-drawn vehicles from Silverdale to Kents Bank).

Morecambe Bay is full of surprises. Cedric relates that while shrimping with his son at night, he would walk in front of the tractor to report on any quicksands. He arranged to signal to his son with a torch if a change of course was necessary. One night, Cedric returned to find his son had had a fright. He was hauling the shrimp net down a channel when he was joined by a porpoise. To him, in the gloom, it had seemed as large as a whale!

*Below: **Cedric Robinson and daughter Jean attend to the fluke nets, which have been set seven miles from land.***

Cedric was fluke-fishing in 1984 when visibility was poor. Having used the railway crossing, he set off to drive his tractor for eight miles across the Sands. He went slowly, intent on leaving a good track with the tyres — a track he could follow on the return. He reached the nets and began to collect a large catch of flukes. The fog became dense and soon the visibility was down to a few yards. Cedric knew that a morning tide doesn't give a fisherman much time; it chases him! He had by no means collected all the flukes but felt that he must return to land without delay. He followed his earlier track as much as possible, choosing the line of a dyke or a gutter if possible. When the coastline suddenly loomed before him, he was relieved to discover he had reached the exact point of departure. The first recognisable object to emerge from the fog was — the railway crossing gate!

If there is a strong wind and a low tide, a sandstorm can develop and greatly reduce visibility. "When it's like that, you're really better at home," one fisherman says. Stormy weather makes fishing difficult. The waves in a channel are too high for the trawl to be kept level. In a blizzard, there is the curious effect of the snow appearing to be approaching the traveller whichever way he looks. Snow settles on the

high banks. "I've been out there when the Bay has been white over," says Cedric. "In shallow water, it can be a mush — like snow broth — and it takes all the tractor marks out."

Most fishermen consider that fog is the worst hazard. Old-time trawlermen from Morecambe, returning home in cloying greyness, heard with thankfulness the clang of hammers against steel at Ward's ship-breaking yard, or the noise made by the hooves of horses on stone setts as the animals drew wagonettes or trams along the promenade. Today, on the Hest Bank side, the sound of inter-city traffic on the railway is as good a guide as you could wish to have in foggy weather!

With metal tractors and trailers involved, a compass can be unreliable. Jack Manning used to have a large type of compass, similar to one used on a lifeboat. He set the compass into the front of a horse-drawn cart and rejoiced because the face of the instrument was luminous. "I could set off in practically any weather and go anywhere." Jack used to work alone when he had a horse and cart. He was out day or night, in "wind, rain, fog, snow or whatever." Having consulted a tide table, he had the fisherman's ready knack of knowing how long the tide-free conditions would last, and where the tide would be at any specific time in every part of the Bay.

Thirty-five years ago, fishermen were catching plaice in various areas. The only plaice to be regularly caught today frequents the area just off the Coast Road, west of Ulverston. Fishermen at Flookburgh caught and sold plaice "before shrimping took off." The average weight was 'three to a pound'. In the autumn of 1985, one man reported netting a plaice at Aldingham. The scales dipped at over 2 lb! Whitebait, which is caught in large quantities, is considered by many to be immature herring. The Morecambe trawlermen were taking whitebait for years before the fishermen at the villages north of the Bay decided it was worth catching. For whitebait, nets are placed on the banks, where an ebb tide moves quickly, and not in a channel. Though moored to a given spot, the whitebait net will float. Luck as well as skill is needed to trap the shoaling fish. "If there's a row of nets, one net might hold four stones of nice clean fish and the other nets can be virtually empty," says Cedric.

Up to the 1914–18 war, a fleet of boats sailed from places north of the Bay to the vicinity of Rampside and Roa Island to collect mussels. A dozen boats were involved, each boat being rather more than 20 feet long, with sail. In those days, the channels were much deeper and the Bay much clearer than they are today. In the early 1920s, when fishing was difficult at Flookburgh, some families moved to the Furness side and made a living collecting mussels.

The old-time fishermen of Morecambe Bay were characters, with distinctive ways and a distinctive form of speech. "Most of them had nicknames, I don't know how they got the names, but it would prove that there was summat about 'em." There were men called *Tarr-o* ("summat to do wi' nets"), *Ganza* (from "gansey"), *Shigger, Clyde, Lion, Gaffer* and his brother *Shir* (from "shire": perhaps they once divided out a fishing catch). Bensons, Butlers and Shaws were well-known families who frequently inter-bred. One branch of the Butler family moved from Flookburgh to live beside the Coast Road. When two fishermen meet, their speech is soon studded with dialect words. There is easy recourse to old terms and expressions. Jack Manning mentions the term *cow-ruck*. "I never thought about it till my sister and I were talking. She happened to mention that one of her sons, who had just got married, needed a *cow-ruck* for the fireside. She was referring to a coal-rake, of course, traditionally used for raking ash from the fire and removing soot from the fire back."

In winter, fishermen walked to the Sands so that they might keep warm, "rather than sit in the cart and be 'starved'." They would have to walk home when the cart was loaded with cockles. Before the days of waterproof gear, men and women wore gaberdine coats which were shower-proof, not rainproof. "If you were out there on a wet day, you got soaked to the skin. If the sun came out, your clothes dried on your back!" In the days before wellingtons and thigh-boots, clogs were frequently worn. Some men wrapped oilskin round their legs. Walter Benson relates that on March 17, the fishermen traditionally left their clogs at the edge of the marsh and went barefooted on to the Sands. "The tale was told that St. Patrick had thrown a stone into the water on the 17th March and made it warmer. Someone said to Jack Stephenson: 'It's St.

Drowned on the Sands: a Commemorative Stone in Cartmel Priory.

Patrick's Day tomorrow, Jack. Thou'll be barefoot after then.' 'Why?' 'Thou knaws, he threw a stone in t'watter to mek it warmer.' Jack said: 'He'll have to throw summat different to a stone before I go barefooted.'" Walter says that fishermen usually took a bottle of cold tea with them to the Sands. They didn't spend much time drinking. If there were a few minutes to spare they would stitch up some bags made from hessian. The bags were used for cockles. "You can't get hessian sacks today; it's all plastic!"

Walter, Jack, ·Cedric and the many other fishermen around Morecambe Bay have tales of impoverishment. When Jack Manning's best friend began work as a farm labourer — he left school at 14 and was hired at Ulverston — he was told: "Aye, I'll tak you on. I'm not going to gie thee so much money, cos if I gie thee a lot of money thou'll only want a lot of time off work to spend it!" A Flookburgh fisherman said: "Our kids won't sit round a table now and pick shrimps. When we were kids, we'd earn a few pence doing this; then we'd go out and buy a few sweets. We were thrilled. Not now. Oh, no. They wouldn't think of it. You couldn't get some women to pick shrimps on a Saturday, for instance. They want to go off shopping . . ."

Fishing, which employed hundreds of people around Morecambe Bay, is now almost finished as a serious commercial practice. The decline began some 10 years ago. "It's a sad story, really. I could see it coming, and nobody else seemed to believe it. The main trouble is that for one reason or another, prices have not kept pace with inflation." For some years, cockles were selling at £6 or £7 a hundredweight. "Now they're £3 a hundredweight. And for that £3, they have to be boiled, whereas in the old days they all went away in the shell. That's all extra work, so they are bringing us less than half what we once got. It doesn't bear thinking about, when you consider that cars or bags of coal or whatever are about seven times what they were then . . ."

Morecambe Bay, with its endless sandbanks and muddy channels, attracts a host of birds. Arguably, the Bay belongs to the birds. In winter, swirling flocks of waders peak at over 70,000 knot and over 40,000 dunlin. These flocks are so dense they look like wraiths of brown smoke being blown along the tideline. The wintering oyster-catchers may number 30,000 birds, many of them refugees from the northern isles. Over 3,000 curlews have assembled at a winter roost near the Kent. Winter "rafts" of eider stay near the mussel beds in the western part of the Bay.

When the impulses of migration have directed bird visitors back to their northern nesting grounds, gulls and

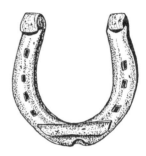

Shoe with "heel"
and "toe" as worn by a
Sands horse.

terns by the thousand settle down to nest on the islands, especially Walney and Foulney. Oystercatchers make territorial claims to tracts of lonely shore and deposit clutches of eggs in shallow scrapes. The shellducks that nest in rabbit holes reappear in due course with new-hatched young — ducklings resembling striped humbugs! — and hope that some of their offspring will survive the attention of hungry gulls.

All creatures adapt themselves to the basic rhythm of Morecambe Bay — to the surge, then ebb of the tide. Twice a day, the Bay is inundated with incalculable quantities of salt water. It is diluted, a little, by freshwater pouring down the rivers from the Lakeland fells . . .

Above: **Fishermen trawling for shrimps in the Ulverston Channel. The photograph was taken in the 1950s.**

Below: **The boatyard at Overton, by the Lune, where "nobbies" used on the Bay were made.**

Left: **Jim Braid and a Lune salmon.** Above: **An estuary boat. Dick Burrow, the last professional fisherman at Arnside.** Bottom, left: **This type of craft sailed in the Lune when drift-netting for salmon.** Below: **At the mouth of the Lune.**

Mouth of the Lune

PINTAIL DRAKE

A HIGH TIDE spills across the road near the *Golden Ball* at Snatchem's, between Lancaster and Overton. The motorist finds another route to take. At Snatchem's, haaf-nets are sometimes seen propped against walls, where they dry out in breezes that are wafted up from the Lune from Morecambe Bay. The road from Overton to Sunderland Point, one and a-half miles in length, regularly goes under water when a flow tide combines with water in the river. Signs at either end of the road proclaim its part-time status. One foggy morning in May, Jim Braid — a local fisherman — arrived just in time to pluck a man from the roof of his van before the tide engulfed him.

Jim's lively mind is a repository of the lore of the tidal Lune. He was born at Overton and "was always fishing." He adds: "I was good at getting wet through. I'd sooner go fishing than go to school." In the event, he left school when he was only 12 years old, in 1917. "They were talking about poor prospects in fishing even then." Jim's first job was on a farm. When he attained his 20th birthday, his father recommended that he should remain in farming. "You'll never make much with fishing," he asserted. But Jim responded to the call of the sea, as had his father and grandfather. He heard them recall their descent from Scottish crofting stock, the type who, on the western seaboard, had derived an income from both land and sea.

Farming the land and river is an ancient twin-occupation at Glasson Dock, Overton and Sunderland Point. The salmon is the principal prey, being sought with haaf-nets, framed by wood and held against the flow of the tide, and with drift nets that are paid out from the stern of a 20 feet long, clinker-built boat. Drift-netting is also called "wammelling." The men work in a strange, remote world of mud and salt water and sky — a world which, however, is rarely quiet, the days being punctuated by bird calls, including the strident *kleep* of the oystercatcher and the wail of the gull.

Jim, and his son David, told us of where the Lune joins the Bay, in the company of other substantial rivers. "When three currents are working out there, it can make a mess of things. We run down to the Lune Deeps but we can't go through that area when the waves are mountains high. The worst conditions are at five to six hours ebb, when it's running the hardest. I'm talking about big tides; when they're coming up the banks . . ." We heard that in 12

Below: **Tom Gardner, a pilot of Sunderland Point**

months, the Lune can change its course by half a mile below Sunderland Point. "There's an old sailing boat down there. It foundered and lost all its crew. One year the river went right past it, but next year the wreck was half a mile from the river." A bore sweeps up the Lune; in some conditions, the wall of water is several feet high.

The Braids clearly remember when the wammel boats were operated with a sail, not an engine. "The original boats were hard to work because they had a transome stern," David told us. "The one we used was called *The Albert*. It had won the regatta at Morecambe in 1908." The best type of wammel boat is one that doesn't draw so much water "for, after all, the salmon do not draw much water!" The fishermen bought white sails but were inclined to have them dipped in all kinds of preservatives so that they would not rot. The dyeing was done at Glasson Dock. It became a matter of "red sails in the sunshine". There was just one sail, a lug, and the fishermen were deft in handling it. "You could put three reefs in. A fisherman would set off at about three hours ebb, get his net out, drift down, use the sail to move across the river or to return to shoot again." The net used from a boat comprises 320 yards of material.

Engines are commonly used today. "You don't need an engine for pulling anything; it's just a matter of getting from A to B to shoot your nets. You are not putting a trawl out. The force of the water spreads out the net, so we like a good breeze." Jim Braid, unsatisfied with the type of boat used on the Lune, as engines were becoming popular went to Mr. Goodall at Sandsend, near Whitby, and had a boat built to a local design. "They fetched it here. Next thing, everybody was wanting a boat like it . . ." Jim's sons took a mould and made about 16 replicas, in fibre glass.

Of the sailing days, Jim recalls: "If there wasn't a wind or the right sort of current, you had to row. When I started using an engine, some of the other fishermen were saying it was all wrong, though when conditions were quiet they were keen enough to put their anchor in and let me tow

Left: **Mending a net at Sunderland Point in the 1950s. The old-type nets were also prone to rotting and some lasted only a few weeks.**

Returning to Sunderland Point after seeking salmon in the Lune.

them." David Braid adds: "If everybody had sails, well — it didn't matter. If only one man had a boat with an engine, he could do whatever he liked. He could get back to the top of the river before the other men got their sails up!"

In wammelling, a fisherman goes out when the tide is "about three hours ebb" and the banks are showing at either side of the channel. "You've got to know where the salmon lie and then see that the nets get to them." Jim remembers when, as a young man, he was annoyed at the quiet acceptance by the older fishermen of what had been done for many years. "Take the net. If it was in a heap, it was soon going rotten. In hot weather, the old type of net lasted for about three weeks." Jim obtained a supply of stuff used for preserving garden fencing and, without letting anyone know of his intentions, he sunk a third of a net into a tub of preservative. The other fishermen soon noticed that this piece of net did not rot as quickly as their nets. "That bit o' net lasted for 28 weeks. I went out with a man one day — when the water was so clear you could see crabs and shrimps moving about. That green bit o' net was close to the boat. The man said: 'Eey, look — there's a salmon.' It was

Below: **Carrying nets and fish ashore after an excursion down the Lune.**

coming alongside the white net towards us. As soon as ever it got to t'green it was caught. It wasn't so long before another salmon had done the same. The other fishermen were soon asking: 'Where do you get the green stuff . . .'"

The season for catching salmon extends from April 1 to the end of August, but the fishermen concentrate most of their activity into a much shorter period. In some six weeks, during a good season, a man can so exhaust himself he would find it difficult to walk straight. Jim remembers when, quite apart from the laborious task of fishing, the men and their families made up their own nets. Many days were spent in "knotting". To carry a haaf-net, draped from an 18 feet long beam, into an icy current, and stay there for a long time, is not the most pleasant of occupations. Jim was often so cold when fishing that he was incapable of closing his hands.

In the days when netting was bulky, salmon could easily see the mesh and avoid the net. So when one of these tough, taciturn fishermen of the Lune spoke about "good fishing weather" they usually meant a strong westerly wind, which would stir and cloud the water, reducing visibility. One Lune drift-netter caught a bottle-nosed dolphin by the mouth. He realised that something was amiss when nearly 30 of the 175 corks on his net went underwater! A salmon does not like slack water; it seeks places where it can feel the flow of the tide or river. "You get most of your salmon under bars of sand, where it's running hard. The law decrees what size mesh should be used, and it is too large to catch all but the largest sea trout. In the last seven or eight years, though, there have been a lot of big sea trout, about five to seven pounds, coming into the Lune. We can stop *them.*" The big sea trout are usually in the river from the middle of May until June. "They cut as pink as salmon."

The Lune fishermen sometimes left their native river to fish further south. The Braids have been down into Liverpool Bay, off Hilbre Island. Jim Braid lost a boat off Fleetwood. He was knocked overboard at night, and the boat kept moving. "In those days, we had double-skin overalls, with a belt. A pocket of air was trapped and I'm sure it saved my life." Jim's early fishing successes, as a lad, were in catching flukes. There was a time, he says, when many local families dined on flukes and little else.

Red sails in the sunset. Above: A photograph loaned by Jim Braid of a party being given a sail on the Lune. Right: Attending to the sail as a "wammel" boat approaches the shore at Sunderland Point. When engines were introduced, a Whitby-type boat was found to be useful. One was brought in by road and 16 fibreglass replicas were made at Overton.

Left: **The ornate entrance to the West End Pier in the 1890s, when Morecambe was nicknamed "Bradford-by-the-Sea".** Bottom, left: **The "Orita" at Morecambe Harbour. She arrived on May 1, 1931. Morecambe had a ship-breaking yard.** Below: **A shrimp-picking competition on the sands at Morecambe in the 1930s.**

OYSTERCATCHER

Morecambe

MORECAMBE is on the Sunset Coast. As a red sun nears the horizon, the effect of the bright light on clouds and the vast expanse of the Bay can be spectacular. It is as though the world is ablaze. The long promenade at Morecambe is a perfect vantage point for the Bay. Those who stride along it find themselves looking again and again at the gleaming sand or water. Incidentally, the name Morecambe was first used for the Bay. It was adopted as the name of the town when the borough was established as recently as 1902.

At the beginning of this century, there was no sea wall at Morecambe, just a huge bank of shingle extending from the Stone Jetty to the Battery (so called because the militia mounted guns here). From Green Street to Hest Bank, the shoreline consisted of salt marsh and similar conditions applied to the Middleton area, south of Heysham. Old people were fond of recalling when wild geese flew here to feed.

The old village of Poulton, with the attendant settlements of Bare and Torrisholme, formed the original borough, and Heysham was added later. The whole has developed into a modern holiday resort, yet those who stand near the Central Pier and see the fishing boats lying at anchor in the channel have a reminder of a once prospering industry. Today there are less than a dozen fishing boats that are used regularly. In place of the graceful "nobbies", wooden craft that had the clean lines of yachts, and were actually sailed to and from the fishing grounds, there are now fibre glass boats, which have a much wider beam. One old Morecambe fisherman calls them "plastic boats"! They are driven through the water by an engine and are totally unsuited to use with sails.

The Morecambe fishermen sail down to areas off Blackpool to fish. Shrimping takes place in the Ulverston channel but, mostly, off Silverdale and below Heysham Head until the Lune Deeps are reached. "They are not much good for our type of fishing, being too deep."

George Mount, of Morecambe, used to claim that an ancestor of his was the only man who had caught a halibut in Morecambe Bay. He towed the fish for four or five miles and landed it at Heysham. On the following morning, a donkey and cart were used to move the great fish to Preston and, with the money from the sale, George bought some coal and carted it back to Morecambe!

The fishermen of Morecambe formed a small, compact community in the area bounded by Marine Road, Lord Street, Poulton Road and Clarence Street — the original Poulton, in fact. It is here that the Morecambe Trawlers, Ltd., continues to operate: a co-operative that was described by the late Professor C.E.M. Joad as "perfect socialism at work"! The organisation was set up for marketing shrimps and fish, a weekly payment being made to the men and the year's profit being shared out on a percentage basis, depending on the individual catches. The company has also provided tackle and waterproof clothing at competitive prices.

Walter Bell made a model of the Morecambe trawler for Morecambe Trawlers, Ltd. (it was placed in the general manager's office). So well made was the model that visitors

21

had a vivid impression of grace and strength, which have been the main qualities of that class of boat down many years. The full-size trawler made by Crossfields of Arnside, was Carvel built, from seven to 10 tons in weight, having a length of 30 to 36 feet, with oak timbers, inch planks, pine decks, carrying pig-iron ballast. In due course this lovely sailing boat was adapted to take an engine.

Eighty yards of cloth had gone into the making of the mainsail, and 25 yards into the topsail. There was once a foresail (18 yards). Sailing across Morecambe Bay was a fine art and the fishermen took great pride in their boats, racing each other to the best fishing grounds. The men also found the time and energy to compete in regattas. Local

*Below: **Morecambe at Holiday-time. In the picture is the famous clock tower.***

trawlers once sought herrings off Maryport and Whitehaven and they were taken southwards to intercept shoals near Southport. The latter end of May, through June and into July, was the time to catch herring. So numerous were the fish that the surplus was carted on to the land to be used as a fertiliser.

A major drawback to fishing from Morecambe is the absence of a harbour. Boats have had to lie in an open channel, where they suffer from being continually exposed to the weather. Westerly gales can cause actual damage. The boats cannot reach home at any state of the tide; they must be back three hours before low water and two hours after. Morecambe Bay shrimps, a speciality, are still boiled on board a trawler. The old-time boiler, which looked incongruous in its position on board a small boat, was known locally as a "talligoram". It held from eight to 12 gallons of water.

Morecambe once owed much of its wealth to the billions of mussels collected at the skeers. Old Dr. Hogarth used to tell of the mussels that formed the great bulk of the shellfish found on the Heysham Skeers. Whereas in Wales, one might find giant mussels — one of which would almost make a meal — at Heysham a mussel rarely grew larger than two and three quarter inches. Unhappily for the fishermen, the sale of these mussels declined: some were found to be sewage-contaminated. Yet in the years between 1900 and 1905, over 2,000 tons of mussels were sent off annually by train from Morecambe.

Bill Baxter, typical of the sturdy fishermen of Morecambe, used to tell us of old-time tragedies in the Bay. His own father, Dick Baxter, was drowned when a sudden gale drove his trawler ashore near Blackpool. Bill himself was out with his brother when heavy seas and a biting wind grounded the trawler at the mouth of the Lune. The two men hurriedly waded ashore; when they returned to the trawler with help they found it had been almost buried by sand and only the mast was in view! Fishermen have told us of the Christmas gale, early this century, when boats were sunk at their moorings. Once, about 200 boats of all kinds were moored off the resort of Morecambe. Though many were made by the Crossfields, some were produced by Ted Woodhouse and Jim Gardner at Overton. (There is a photograph of the Overton enterprise in this book).

Above: **Morecambe trawlers lying at anchor among ice floes near the Stone Jetty. The town has never had a proper harbour and boats have also been badly** exposed to westerly gales. Below: **Low-tide reveals the graceful, yacht-like form of a Morecambe trawler, the type made by Crossfields of Arnside.**

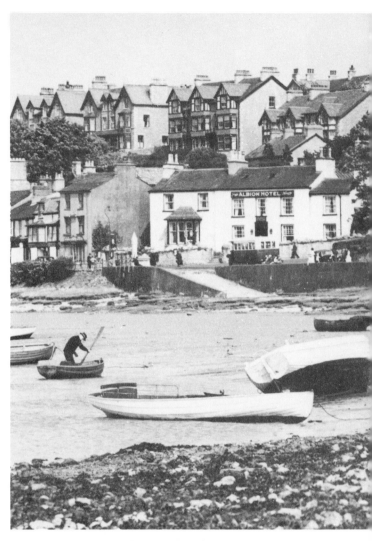

Left: **Westerly gale in the Kent estuary. Waves bombard the sea wall near the "Ship" Inn.** *Above:* **Arnside in the 1950s.**

Estuary of the Kent

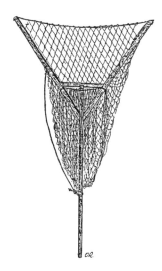

NET FOR SALMON.

DESMOND BURROW, whose home at Arnside overlooks the Kent, regularly watches the bore, the turbulent forward edge of a tide. He has never lost his fascination with the daily transformation scene provided by the restless sea. "If you look at the estuary at low tide, you see a vast area of sand and mud. It looks like the Sahara, with the addition of a little trickle of water running across it. Then you hear the buzzer blow to warn people of the tide's approach. If it's a spring tide, some 10 minutes after the sound of that buzzer has died away, you'll see the bore appear, roaring by at a speed of around nine knots. In two hours, the estuary is full of water. There's water right up to the promenade and across to Grange. Visitors, getting out of their cars when the tide is high, look at the estuary and say one to another: 'What's the name of this lake?'" In two hours, millions of gallons of water have entered the estuary and, before long, it has drained. There has been a return to sand and mud.

The tidal bore breaks its back against the famous railway viaduct. "To get a good photograph, I usually stand with my camera on Ashmeadow Corner," says Desmond Burrow. He mentioned to us the fairly rapid siltation of the estuary, which at times reduces the Kent to something of a trickle. "It may be possible to wade across it in places, but don't try to do this, because high tides and heavy rain can change the situation overnight and there are quicksands — soft spots that form where the sand has been lubricated by water. Sand that doesn't get a current of water about it can lie undisturbed for years. It becomes as hard as iron . . ."

In a very cold spell, ice floes are seen in the estuary and the tide pushes some of them against the viaduct. "The railway authority used to have men out at night trying to break up the ice with long poles." Up to the 1950s, when only one main arch was open to the surge of the tide, it was decided to open up others. (Previously, a diver was employed, at least once a year, to reinforce the base of a pier by lagging it with bags containing quick-setting cement).

Desmond's late father, Richard, was the last full-time fisherman at Arnside. Hearing that a big ship was being broken up at Barrow, Richard purchased a ship's lifeboat for £5. A heavy boat, having been built purely for use in an emergency, it was named *Girl Pat*. Father towed it out into the Bay with a party of sea anglers, their tackle and bait, also six crates of beer! Desmond recalls: "By lunchtime on a glorious summer's day, all you would see would be six pairs of feet extending over the gunwails, also six rods protruding from the boat. The men had drunk enough beer to make them sleepy." On their return to the shore, Richard Burrow would sell the anglers some flounders he had caught, and they took these fish home, where the wives of the anglers were impressed. They did not object when the men suggested they might have another day's fishing from Arnside!

Up to the 1939–45 war, salmon-netting was prohibited on the estuary of the Kent, yet salmon were caught. As one fisherman said: "If salmon found their way into our nets, we weren't going to throw them back!" Just after the war, netting was allowed. "They started off with the haaf-net, which had a beam of 14 feet. They stood breast-deep in water, as they do down the Lune, and they fished both tidal currents. I remember Dad getting one of those nets and trying to operate it. The Kent is a much shallower river than the Lune and the net proved to be unwieldy. Dad elected to go for a lave-net, a smaller version, being something like a large landing net, with four and a-half inch mesh. You just stood in the water with it . . ."

The river Kent was allocated only six licences, though everybody wanted a salmon licence. "Each licence was endorsed so that two men could operate with it, but only six had to be at the river at one time. The heaviest salmon that Dad ever got was a 29-pounder."

Many acres of sea thrift bloom on the shore between Arnside and Silverdale. The channel of the Kent, which was for long on the Grange side, has now come close inshore again. Years ago, boats could tie up at the Cove, Silverdale, but the shipping trade was declining by 1850 as the Cove silted. An ambitious scheme to reclaim the Silverdale Sands was put forward in 1864, and from near Jenny Brown's Point can be seen the remains of a substantial wall

that extended seaward for about a mile. It has been buried for many years.

Arnside Sailing Club has revived some of the glories of the past, when boats were as common as vehicles. A Directory of 1849 states that Arnside Sands "are covered one hour with ships and another with carriages and pedestrians." The old sport of punt-gunning was carried out in the daylight hours, always at low water, aimed at bagging some of the wintering waterfowl, including the grey geese that appeared after a 500-mile journey from Iceland. More commonly slain were the various species of duck. "We don't get a lot of greylags in the estuary, maybe one or two hundred," says Desmond Burrow. "At one time, you reckoned that they would appear on October 22, give or take a few days on either side of that date. Latterly, they have not been quite as regular in their habits. The punt-gunners went looking for duck, particularly the 'little wigeon'."

In the 1890s, the Sharpe family of Halton Hall, Lancaster, kept a 24 feet long punt for use on the Kent estuary. The gun (usually referred to as a "cannon") had a bore of 1½ inches and fired 1½lb. of shot. A typical entry in the game book was this, for September 23: "Dick Storey and I launched Arnside at 1-30. Down to Winster. High water 5-30. Height 11ft 4″, calm day. Lots of birds but no chance." The object was to drift down the channel in such a way that birds accepted the punt as they might accept a floating log. There were usually two men in a punt, a man at the back controlling its movement and another attending to the "cannon". There would be little point in shooting unless a punt-gunner got to within 60 or 70 yards of the birds. In the 1943–44 winter, a record shot of 33 wigeon from a punt-gun was broken a fortnight later with a bag of 42 wigeon. "Mind you, the first shot was a flying shot; the second a sitting shot."

For many, the pleasure is in merely watching the birds. Grey geese, rising from Meathop Marsh, make patterns in the sky on their way to roost on the high banks in the Bay. Pink-footed, white-fronted barnacle and brent geese have been periodically observed. Shelduck waddle on the wet sands. Curlew probe for food and add their bubbling call to the wild chorus. Kent estuary also holds a large stock of oystercatchers, the ubiquitous "sea-pie".

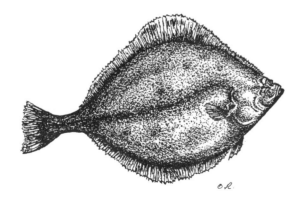

A Morecambe Bay fluke.

Royal Carriage Ride

Above: **The Duke of Edinburgh, with Cedric Robinson beside him, approaches Kents Bank at the end of the historic cross-bay carriage drive in May, 1985.**

FOR THE CROSSING of Morecambe Bay by a group of carriages, on May 30, 1985, weeks of planning were undertaken. The first carriage would be driven by the Duke of Edinburgh. For Cedric, there was a regular consultation of tides and tide tables. Scarcely a weather forecast was missed. Would the weather clear in time for the Sands to harden enough for narrow-wheeled vehicles? Inquiries were being made around the village of Silverdale for a suitable meeting place for the drivers and the vehicles carrying the horses and carriages. After several visits to the area by Cedric, and later by Mr. Hugh Cavendish and Mr. Lea from Holker Hall, the ideal place was found at the Stone Bower Fellowship Home for the Elderly Disabled, in Cove Road. Bernard Wood, manager of the Home, willingly gave permission. From here, there was good access to the shore. Straight ahead, running over the grassy marshland and out towards the sands, was a good firm route, which years earlier, had been laid with "hard core" for the benefit of tractors and trailers loaded with sea-washed turf.

At the time of the visit to Silverdale, the tides were low. They had been low for a few days. The Sands near the marshland dried out, giving the false impression that they were safe. Several days later, when Cedric re-visited Silverdale, the weather had changed, the tides had risen in height and he found the whole area was unsuitable. He did have an alternative route in mind. It was an uneven way, across the marsh, with deep holes and nasty gullies, ending with a pretty steep drop. Although the depth of this varied

within a foot or so in places, the sand level must have been at least four feet lower than the marsh. Someone with a J.C.B. mechanical digger was needed to fill the holes and do a patching-up job here and there. He could also make a wide ramp with sand. The owners of the marsh (R.S.P.B.) readily gave permission for this to be done. David Singleton from Tewitfield, Carnforth, and his son, Peter, satisfactorily carried out the work.

Cedric knew that it would be a waste of time if this work was done too soon, for the tides would wash the sand away. He decided that the work must be carried out on the day before the Carriage Crossing, when the tides were at their lowest. "We had to gamble on the weather and hope that it would stay fine."

Tetley Walker, the North-West brewer, was sponsoring both the Kent Crossing and the Holker Driving Trials. There had so far been no official announcement that the Duke of Edinburgh would take part in the drive over the sands. The Police, the Coastguard, John Duerdon from Arnside and Don Shearer from Walney, were informed of any progress. It was Tetley Walker's fourth year of sponsorship of the events at Holker Hall, and it coincided with their tenth anniversary.

When it was officially announced that the Duke of

Edinburgh was to take part in the drive over the sands, lots of people were concerned about the horses, thinking it was too dangerous. What would happen if some of them were to go down in quicksands? Cedric assured inquirers that the horses would come to no harm, and would be all the better for the drive. When horses were used regularly by the Flookburgh fishermen, including himself, although it was hard work for them at times, they were always fed well, and the salt water did them good, improving their joints. There was never a poor horse to be seen out on the Bay!

Cedric spent long, anxious hours on the Sands, plotting a safe route, only to find the sands were shifting at every tide. "We were hoping and praying for some kind of miracle to happen out there, to improve the conditions, and to make the drive possible." In truth he was feeling a little despondent, having spent long hours out on the Sands with very little to show for it. There was no point in marking out a route if the place chosen one day was to be impossible on the following day. It was estimated that the river Kent moved between 400 and 500 yards each day.

Cedric organised the cutting of the "brobs" used for marking out the route. "I was lucky to have good friends, on both sides of the Bay, who were only too keen to give me a hand." On the Silverdale side, George Riley, of Bolton-le-Sands, Kath Alty and Dick Proctor gave their help. John Duerdon, and several of his Coastguard auxiliaries, came as far as the river Kent with Cedric on the final stage of marking out the route, and John Barber, Cedric's son-in-law Chris, and Cedric himself, marked other stretches of the route. A search for "brobs" was initiated. At Guides Farm, until recently, there had been a good length of hedge composed of overgrown laurel bushes. Cedric cut the hedge to mark out the river crossings during the summer walks and also to provide markers on the cockle grounds in the murky winter months. Unfortunately, some enthusiastic road workers, while laying large pipes for a new sewage system, had lopped the laurels almost to the ground. Another source of supply had to be found.

The weather for the Great Day was heartening. There would be a change to fine weather with the arrival of a high pressure system. "Our prayers had been answered! This was the news we had been waiting for, and now it was 'all systems go'." Cedric decided to meet up with his helpers and

also Barbara Stothart and her brother, Judge Sandy Temple, who were both carriage drivers. They offered to look at the route and in due course to give a hand. Ian Brodie, a teacher from Garstang, also gave help. Cedric needed to find a good friend with lots of laurel bushes who would allow pieces to be cut for marking out the route on the Grange-over-Sands side of the Bay. Mrs. E. Williams, of Kents Bank, came to the rescue.

"It took us two days to mark out the route from Silverdale side, using 200 brobs, to a point almost half way across the Bay where the sand rose to a higher level and was safe and sound. Many of the 'brobs' had to be replaced after each tide as the river Kent moved its course. The route chosen was not a direct one; it snaked to and fro, avoiding large areas of shifting sands. This also added to the mileage, which was now approximately six miles."

On the night before the Royal Coach Crossing, Cedric went to bed knowing that he had done everything humanly possible to make the crossing pleasureable and safe. It would be an advantage to make an early start on the following morning. He and his helpers set out from Guides Farm at 3.30am, traversing sands which he knew well and carefully choosing a route so that markers could be put in the sand on the return journey. The first priority was to reach the river Kent for a final check. Cedric recalls: "You would never believe a river could behave in such a way. It had moved at least 150 yards from the markers put in the sand the day before. What I didn't realise until we were in the river, and testing the sand for firmness, was that the route had become firmer. All we had to do now was to move some of the original markers and replace the ones which had been washed away." They turned for home, completing the marking of the route to Kents Bank Station. The day dawned with a clear sky. "As we watched the sun rise, we knew then that we were in for a perfect day."

At Guides Farm, as the day progressed, all was bustle and activity. Cedric's wife and daughter were baking, having decided to lay on a buffet for helpers and friends

*Right: **The Duke of Edinburgh controls four spirited Cleveland Bays during the crossing of the Kent Sands, not forgetting the river. The crossing was made in bright, though warm, conditions.***

when all would meet back at the house after the crossing. So many Press representatives arrived that it was arranged to use two tractors and trailers and one pick-up truck for transport on the Sands to a safe observation area. Cedric always carries his stick when testing the Sands on organised walks, but this day he left it behind, he had, instead, a Coastguard's walkie-talkie.

At Silverdale, large numbers of people were basking in the glorious sunshine. Thousands had flocked to the foreshore to glimpse the Duke. Initially, the route was indicated by white-painted wooden pegs, in a continuous line, almost parallel with the shoreline, from the Cove towards the cottages, to meet up with the old "cockle road". "There was nothing the Silverdale people would have liked better than to have seen the Duke of Edinburgh, his magnificent team and the other carriages driving along the road, down through the village and onto the shore. The police said they could not guarantee maximum security to cover this, so an alternative had to be found."

Bernard Wood, the manager of Stone Bower, and all the patients, were pleased when it was agreed that the organised drive should start from their grounds. As the horse boxes were arriving, the one carrying the Duke's magnificent Cleveland Bays was parked as close as possible to the Home to allow patients to watch the preparations.

Cedric decided that the outfits would be lined up in two groups of six, side by side, but allowing safe distances between them. The Duke's carriage would be on the right flank of the front line. The second line of six would follow at least 50 yards behind, to the left. "I thought this order should be kept until we were at least half way across the Bay and clear of the low-lying, watery areas. Once we reached the higher ground, the Sands would be much firmer and quite safe so that we could then follow, one carriage behind the other, just slightly offset, in the same way the fishermen used to do, including myself, when we followed the Sands with horse and cart."

The drivers and their passengers climbed aboard their carriages. Cedric was asked to climb up on the front seat and sit alongside the Duke. The drive started at 3.30pm, with the Duke leading the procession, flanked by policemen on horseback. He was in charge of a team of four magnificent Cleveland Bays, and behind him came 11 other carriages, with two outriders bringing up the rear.

Large crowds lined the route, with everyone cheering and clapping as the Duke's carriage came into view. From where Cedric was sitting, it looked as if everyone who could hold a camera had brought one along with them on that beautiful day.

As he watched the Duke of Edinburgh handling his team, Cedric sensed the power and intelligence of the four Cleveland Bays. "The Duke spoke frequently to them, calling each one by name, as we made our way down to the shore. This took us only a matter of minutes. Large crowds had gathered on the marsh and it was here that we lost the route, at the start! I soon realised the mistake, and pointed it out to the Duke. Luckily, among the crowds of people and all the parked cars, was a space wide enough to allow him to manoeuvre his team around and pick out the route. The other drivers following in single file. People who were standing in that area obscured our view of the small markers, and as the marsh was a jig-saw of gullies, it wasn't easy to pick out the route."

At the most awkward and narrow drains, the organisers had laid planks of wood to prevent injury to the horses. As the first one was approached, Cedric instinctively held the side of the carriage. "I thought to myself: 'I know what is going to happen here: the horses will jump this'. They did, but after negotiating the first one, they took the others in their stride, as the Duke spoke quietly to them. Then they just walked on, ignoring the boards and the crowds around them. It was more than I could say for some of the other horses. Some of the drivers had great difficulty in getting their teams to cross the boards. The horses reared and almost overturned the carriages."

Eventually, the party was on firm ground near the Sands, though three noisy helicopters upset the horses. "Ahead now, lining both sides of the track we were following, was the largest crowd of people I had ever seen." The Sands route was now clearly marked with "brobs" and for the first half of the drive these made it easier for the drivers to follow. "It was here that some difficulty arose. The spectators surged on to the sands, following the Duke's carriage. Lots of people ran into the path of the horses. When we drew to a halt for a few moments, it seemed chaotic. I could see only two other carriages, as they came

forward to the line-up. One was being driven by Judge Temple, from Yealand (his passenger was Mr. Hugh Cavendish, of Holker) and the driver of the other carriage was Mrs. Barbara Stothert, sister of Judge Temple. The others were completely lost in the crowds."

In due course, Cedric could see that everyone was ready. Prince Philip then told his team of horses to walk on. "Cheers went up as we left the crowds behind, and soon the horses were asked to trot on. It wasn't easy for the carriage drivers, as you can imagine, but two Coastguard vehicles were on hand to make sure none of the enthusiastic crowd wandered too far. Nothing had been rehearsed. With horses of different sizes and temperament, there was difficulty at first in keeping distances. At times they were far too close for comfort. As we progressed into the bay, the drivers became accustomed to it — and the horses seemed to enjoy the experience."

The river Kent was crossed at a trot, as the water was fast flowing and axle deep. "It was here that one of the lead horses pulling the Royal carriage decided that it did not like the look of one of the "brobs" in the river, and shied away rather sharply to the left. A word from the Duke soon straightened him up. These Clevelands were very powerful

*Above: **A group following the Duke's carriage across the Sands. In the picture (left) is an outfit handled by Judge Temple, who is accompanied by Mr. Hugh Cavendish of Holker Hall.***

horses but the Duke — being the splendid horseman he is — controlled them with his quietly-spoken commands."

Where the route was marked clearly, it was possible for Cedric to look around and keep an eye on the other carriages. Shortly after the river crossing, there was another stretch of water, slightly deeper, but with less flow than in the main river. This stretch was deeper over to the left and it shelved off. "My worry was that if the smallest pony on the drive, a grey Welsh mountain pony, just over eleven hands high, was to be on the left of the other carriages, he would have to swim. Looking back over my shoulder, I saw that he was in among the other horses and doing well, with neck outstretched. The drivers and passengers would have got a little wetting!"

Cedric described to the Duke the nature of the river Kent and especially its fickle ways. He also spoke about the quicksands. "He was interested and I found him very easy

31

to talk to. I had to ask him to slow the pace of his powerful team. We were leaving the other carriages, with smaller horses and ponies, well behind."

Ahead was one more stretch of water, which until recently had been the river Kent. This was wide but shallow. On the far bank, awaiting the Duke and the cavalcade of horse-drawn vehicles, was the media. "Our

Below: **Placing "brobs" in advance of the Royal crossing.**

32

approach to this watercourse was in wide formation, with the horses moving briskly at the trot. The horses and carriages entered the water at the same time, trying hard to keep formation. I had happy memories of shrimping with horse and cart as I heard the horses hooves and the swish of the carriage wheels."

The party was now travelling over good, firm sand. From here on, the horses were asked to slow to walking pace, and it was possible for the carriages to follow one behind the other. The sand rose to a higher level and, with a combination of much lower tides, a dry warm breeze and brilliant sunshine, the views around had great clarity. "We were now looking at the Bay at its best."

As the Duke told his team to trot on, Cedric was hoping that they would not arrive at Kents Bank Station before time, for there had been negotiations with British Rail to ensure maximum safety over the railway crossing. They had laid boards over the railway lines at the point where the horses and carriages were to cross. Occasionally the pace slowed, as dykes and gullies were crossed, but as the Royal cavalcade came into view of the thousands who had gathered on the foreshore at Kents Bank, the team of Shire horses belonging to Tetley Walker, were waiting to be driven in the procession behind the Duke's carriage. "It had been agreed that from here to the shore, all the horses would come in at a steady trot. As we approached the crowds, towards the end of this historic crossing, cheers went up. We had conquered the bay and its unpredictable moods and quicksands. This was certainly the most memorable day of my life. The Duke doffed his cap and remarked that, apart from the noise of the helicopters, the trip had been delightful."

As the Duke drove on the road beside the Kents Bank Post Office, he chose to halt his team of horses under the shade of some trees near to Priory Lane. Cedric climbed down from the Royal Carriage, his work over . . . After the Bay crossing, the Horse Trials took place in Holker Park. Cedric and his wife Olive were there. "We were standing at the back of the crowd of people when the Duke of Edinburgh passed. He caught sight of me and waved, calling: 'Have you recovered from the ordeal, Mr. Robinson?' It was a pleasant surprise for us to receive, in due course, a letter of thanks from Buckingham Palace."

Grange-over-Sands

GUIDE'S HOUSE IN CART LANE.

THE HOME of the Sands Guide, at the end of Cart Lane, is an attractive old farm, with land round about. It was even more attractive before the railway arrived, with the lines laid on the edge of the Bay. Today, from the front door, you have to stand on tip-toe to see all the Bay. When Guides Farm was built, there were no other dwellings in the immediate area.

Grange-over-Sands is largely a 19th and early 20th century creation — a town of attractive, large houses, set on a hillside, with breath-taking views of the flow and ebb of the tide; of Holme Island, Arnside Knott and Morecambe, which at night beads the skyline with orange lights. (It was

to avoid confusion with an older name, Grange-in-Borrowdale, that little Grange was elevated to Grange-over-Sands. The idea was promoted by Canon H.R. Smith, who was the incumbent from 1858 to 1888).

The railway did at least fix the shoreline at Grange, for the tides had run as far as the main street. The old Grange Council made tremendous strides in beautifying the new town. In 1905, when Anthony Benson was appointed head gardener, not one plant was grown by the Council and shrubs, mostly laurels, dominated the public ground. Mr. Harold Porritt, who lived at Netherwood, paid for the erection of a promenade and Col. Porritt tried unsuccessfully to have it extended to Kents Bank. At one time there were two piers at Grange. A local resident told us that when he was a youngster he dived from the big wooden baulks of a pier. "Nobody bothered to maintain the pier. Eventually, it fell to pieces."

When the Kent channel was near the promenade at Grange, there was rejoicing among those who catered for visitors by hiring out boats. The large Burrow family were involved in both boating and catching fish. "When the tide was out, there was still enough water in the river for boats. People, hiring them on a glorious June morning, would go

*Left: **Cartmel Priory at the turn of the century. It was this monastic institution which established a Grange by the Sands.***

33

Grange-over-Sands Pier.

Grange-over-Sands from U...

Above: **Victorian visitors look with interest at the activity around Clare House pier at Grange. (There were two piers at this popular resort).** *Top, right:* **The Main Street at Grange.** *Right:* **Boating in the Kent Channel at Grange-over-Sands in the 1890s.**

34

as far as Holme Island." Crossfields, of Arnside, made a large number of rowing boats. In 1914, Richard Burrow collected a craft for which he paid £3.10s. Such a boat was made of larch, on an oak frame, and was varnished. "The local fishermen used to daub them up with paint or put gas tar on them," we were told. One man said to the proud owner of a new boat he was collecting: "Ay, lad; it's great. You want to take it home and tar it. Yon boat'll then last forivver."

Grange benefits from its sheltered position. The "Torquay of the North" has an especially mild climate. "We don't get the extremes you find further inland, even four or five miles away," said a local shopkeeper. A newcomer has had difficulty whenever the television news carried pictures of snow in "Cumbria". Friends in the south know that Grange is in Cumbria. They ring up or write anxiously inquiring about the plight of the family! Local children are warned not to play on the shore which, being rather more mud than sand, is subjected to the whims of the river Kent, with its fickle ways and its ominous "soft spots".

The bathing pool is vital on a coastline where bathing can be dangerous. "It's a lovely pool when the summer sun's been on it for a day or two." It is at Grange that Gordon Handslip has owned a grocer's shop for many years. Gordon has celebrated his 90th birthday. Taking up bay cross-walking in middle-age, he went on to complete the crossing well over 120 times!

The railway station at Grange is a stylish building. The quirks of the old Furness Railway Company are evident in the architectural detail, including convoluted downspouts and an elegant wrought iron-and-glass canopy. Leave the station and you immediately see the first of three massive hotels — the *Grand, Grange* and *Netherwood*. They stand well clear of the road, for they were built to be seen in their extensive, tree-decked settings. Grange's ornamental gardens, a retreat for visitors, are the home of plants that need a mild climate and sustain a varied throng of waterfowl.

Gordon Handslip remembers when, in about 1930, his family took in holiday visitors, providing them with accommodation. Handslip hospitality extended to cooking the food the visitors brought. There was a charge of 28s a week for one person, 35s a week for two. There was a

regular boat service between Grange and Morecambe. Grange folk went "on the morning tide" and stopped at Morecambe all day; the Morecambe folk came "with the tide" and had to go back with it. So they had scarcely time to look around. Local men rowed daring visitors into the Bay to meet the bore which formed with the onset of the tide. It was a novel experience.

The cross-bay walkers, supervised by Cedric, negotiate sand and water on their way to a landfall at Kents Bank. They are a familiar sight at Grange in the warmer months. Cedric tells of a first crossing of the season — on May Day — when conditions were anything but springlike. "Living at Grange, where we are sheltered, I always go to the start of the walk at Hest Bank prepared for cooler, windier conditions. At Hest Bank, it was blowing a gale. I sat there, waiting, and then one or two coaches came along, and people stepped off flimsily clad and shivering. We gathered round for a chat. It was so bad I could have called it off, but they said they would like it to go on."

Looking out from Hest Bank to the lower part of the Bay was awesome. Waves were crashing in and visibility was poor. The Keer was "pretty deep". At the high sands, Cedric looked round at the party and saw that everybody was covered with sand — completely covered. "Once we got near Silverdale, which is normally a stopping place, some of the walkers were so cold and miserable they just couldn't go on. I directed half the walkers on a safe route into the village. The remainder followed me, and for a while we walked into the teeth of a gale. It came on raining. The storm blotted out all familiar features. We stopped so that I could get my bearings. Two or three inches of flood water was being blown across the Bay. The people thought that it was the tide coming in! At the river, I looked for the 'brobs' I had used to mark it on the previous day. Normally, they would have been visible on either side of the water. This day they were standing in water and so I knew it was going to be a deep crossing. The water was above waist deep. One lady took cramp and had to be carried all the way to the shore." Everyone found pleasure in recalling this difficult crossing.

In his capacity as fisherman, Guide to the Sands and auxiliary coastguard, Cedric has had some unusual assignments, including offering help to a party of Roundheads on a special anniversary ride across the Bay to Arnside, where

Grange-over-Sands, showing the pier at Crown Hill and the channel of the Kent.

they joined battle with the Cavaliers on the shore at White Creek. He has also accompanied a walker with a Chinese wheelbarrow, complete with sail, on a preliminary test for possible use as transport in the desert.

Cedric recalls taking a small group of walkers from his home in Cart Lane over to Chapel Island. "It was a glorious day — so nice that everyone left their clothing in the cars at Sandgate. We set off wearing next to nothing. I was a little bit more sensible: I carried a jersey over my arm. We decided to spend a couple of hours on Chapel Island. There were one or two elderly people in the group, also lots of youngsters. On the far side of Chapel Island, the interest was a natural swimming pool; it was such a hot day . . . The others walked round the island, looking at the wildlife. When we decided it was time for home, we set off on what still looked to be a beautiful day.

"We got about a quarter of a mile, and were facing towards Sandgate and home when we heard a noise like the tide coming — or even the passage of a steam train. A storm was coming up the Bay. There was no way we were going to get clear of it! When it hit us, the rain was coming like bullets, so fast and fierce that all landmarks and our sandmarks were lost. What was nice dry sand suddenly became about two inches of sodden sand. Everything merged into one. It was a funny sensation because there was lightning as well. There was no way we could get out of it." (Cedric's wife recalls seeing the storm from the house. "On that day I was washing. I hung the clothes out to dry. One moment, the washing was still and the next moment it was being blown high in the air. I could hardly get the clothes off the line").

Cedric carries a whistle, "but it didn't make any difference because although we were only a small group we had broken up into three groups. Everybody held hands and walked with their heads down. What seemed like an age was only a matter of minutes. The storm passed. I blew the whistle. We all got together — and had a talk about our frightening experience."

Bandstand and cafe on the Promenade at Grange.

Grange's stylish railway station.

Fishermen of Flookburgh

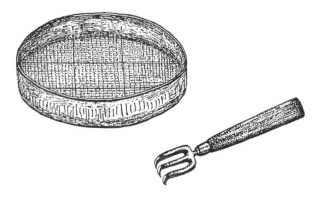

COCKLE RIDDLE (ABOVE) AND CRAAM.

DOMINATING the parish church at Flookburgh is a weather vane in the shape of a fish — a gilded fish. We asked an old man about it. "Well, there's some say it's a dolphin," he said, scratching his head. "I wouldn't like to say. But I know one thing — it isn't a fluke!" The fish on the church resembles an angler fish *(Lophius Piscatorius)*. Cedric has caught many young fish in his white bait nets. The principal fishing village to the north of Morecambe Bay, Flookburgh is situated over a mile from the shore. For many years, its men used horses and carts (now tractors and trailers made from car chassis) as they "followed the Sands". Few full-time fishermen remain. Retired men talk about the hard life that was, and one of them told us of the 1930s, a time of industrial depression, when his father left fishing for a while and went to work in the steel works at Barrow-in-Furness. When the war came, and with it a need for home-produced food, fishing in the Bay throve as never before.

Half a century ago, Flookburgh was an independent, characterful place. A typical cottage had a spartan character. "There were no carpets in the houses — just a bit o' coconut matting here and there. Nearly all the houses had black-lead fireplaces and plain wooden furniture. You'd take the main carpet up for the shrimp-picking season. I remember when nails were driven into a large beam and used when making or repairing nets. Another fisherman drove two big nails in a wall, and when times were slack, or the weather none so good, he'd sit for many an hour 'knitting' nets. In those days, nets were made of cotton, then dipped in the sort o' tar they used to patch up the road. I remember seeing an old bath half full of tar. A chap dropped a bundle of netting into it on a rope; he gave it a good soak, then pulled it up and let it drain. A net like

that never really dried out. Even when you thought it was dry and you'd take it to the sand, you always got clarted up."

Many a fire was kept alive with peat taken from Holker mosses. It was stored in a peat house, which stood separate from the main house. It was here that one lady spent hours filleting fish at all times of the year. "It wasn't really fit for her to be there, for the peat house didn't have a proper door. The door was slatted, like a gate. It was terribly draughty. Yet she sat there, on and off, for years; filleting flukes for her dad, and then he'd hawk 'em round the village." The main outbuilding was also a coal house and here stood a boiler with an iron set-pot, which had a dual role, being used for boiling shrimps and doing the weekly wash!

At Flookburgh, they still talk about Old Tom Wilson, who caught a porpoise in a net set for much smaller fish. He brought the porpoise back to Flookburgh, cut it up and "rendered it down" to make "porpoise oil". People complained about the smell. "There were a lot of funny smells in the village then, but when Tom was making that porpoise oil the place wasn't fit to live in. Then it didn't matter what your ailment was, you had to have some porpoise oil. They were just as keen on it as Italians with olive oil. James Butler had an off-licence down the main street. When he sold the shop, they found some old-fashioned stone jars. They said they had been filled with

Leaving the Sands for the marsh road at Flookburgh.

porpoise oil — and the stuff had 'eaten' right through the 'stone'!"

Nobody really caught a porpoise. "They catched therselves." They saw the net, of course, and they "stopped and messed about till the water left them and they were stranded. We had a baulk that was set behind Humphrey Head; it stopped two porpoise . . . There was a wedding in the village that day. Our Tommy come and said — 'there's summat yonder'. The dolphins were on their sides; one was almost 'past it' by then. There wasn't anything we could do for them. For a guess, each would weigh half a ton. We had to leave 'em."

Walter Benson, who started going to the Sands in 1936, with his uncle, Bill Hodgson, recalls that the occupation was mainly cockling then. Another uncle went only at week-ends; at other times he was hawking fish, fruit and vegetables. Flookburgh's pre-occupation with trading began when men hawked cockles and flukes. "Then one or two of them arranged for boxes of herrings to be sent to them, adding to the variety. They started selling some of the produce from their gardens. Then we had a fruit chap or two came — wholesale fruiterers, that is — and before you knew it there were five wholesale fruiterers coming to Flookburgh and over 30 men going out to sell produce every morning. Old Austin cars, adapted for carrying goods, were ideal tradesmen's vehicles.

Not until the 1940s did shrimping become the first consideration. Good horses were a vital part of the fishermen's working routine — Jack Manning recalled details of the stable that adjoined the house at Flookburgh in which he grew up. "It held a lot of home-made tackle. The *skel-booses* (barriers between stalls), knocked up from odd pieces of wood, rose to a height of about six feet. The horse

*Left: **A Family Effort. In the picture, sorting whitebait at Cart Lane, Grange, are three members of the Robinson family** — Olive, wife of Cedric, their daughter Jean and, representing a third generation, Gladys. Right: Harold Manning and his father, Jim, riddling and sorting shrimps; the shrimps have been spread on hessian.*

Above: **Jean Robinson (now Mrs. Jackson) carries a Jumbo, the wooden implement used by Morecambe Bay fisherman to coax cockles to the surface in the Bay. On this occasion, the Jumbo could only be used at low water mark, and then not for long. Intensely cold conditions had covered virtually the whole area with ice.**

was fed a good and varied diet — hay, oats and bran." His family had about six acres of land and could grow grass for conversion into hay for the winter. The grass was mowed by a local farmer. Fishermen who did not own land had to buy hay from farmers, collecting the hay in their own carts. Some fishermen rented small fields in which to graze their horses.

Horses were bought mainly from dealers. Every fisherman was alert to a local bargain, such as a horse no longer needed by a farmer or by the owner of horse-cabs at Morecambe. Many a horse that spent years pulling cabs along Morecambe promenade had a new lease of life on the Sands. A few horses were bought at the old fairs at Brough and Appleby, but you needed to have made every mistake in buying or selling horses to have the confidence to deal in places such as those, where most of the traders were sharp-witted "travellers". Longevity in a horse was taken for granted. Old Thomas Wilson, of Flookburgh, owned a horse which he kept until it was 19 years old. He then sold it at Ulverston to a man who kept it to haul a milk dray in the town.

Fishermen used the type of horse-drawn cart made for farmers by local joiners. It was two-wheeled, standing well clear of the ground, the big wheels giving a horse every help by reducing the amount of drag as it drew the cart through deep water. When the number of joiners capable of making carts declined, the fishermen replaced their old or damaged carts with those bought at farm sales.

When cockling, a fisherman did not need his horse for an hour or two. Jack Manning relates that to avoid having a chilled horse, the fisherman would remove it from the shafts, tip up the cart, having regard to the wind direction and stand the horse where it derived shelter from the weather. The animal was provided with a nose bag containing hay. There might be half a ton of cockles on the cart when it was drawn off the Sands.

Walter Benson says that there have been more "sieges" (mirings) with the tractors than with horses. A tractor engine would start vibrating and, before a man could look around, the tractor would be sinking. Ideally, four or five tractors should be mustered, with a separate line from each, to pull the stricken tractor out of the soft spot. "Latterly, they've got to putting 50 gallon barrels on for

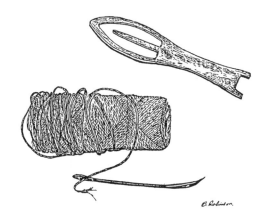

Knitting "needle" of wood used for making and mending nets (above). Packing needle and twine used for securing hessian sacks (below).

buoyancy; they seem to get away with that." In the horse days, a fisherman with a mired horse started digging with a spade, though "sipings" (drainage of water into a hole) were troublesome. One horse made a special effort "when it got a bit o' water in its eyes" and it struggled free. "It was all cramped up," its owner recalls. "Off it set, in its tin-pot way, for home. It didn't want to know me for quite a while and then I got its confidence back."

A dyke called Holy Well Dyke — "we call it Ally Well" — near Humphrey Head could be difficult. One man "struck in wi' t'hoss" sooner than he should have done. He always said that he had a good hoss, "a real 'un, that 'ud swim in watter wi' just its lugs out." This time, the horse was indeed swimming, and the water was so deep it floated the baskets from the cart and bore them away. The old fisherman who was in charge shouted to the horse: "Goo' lad, goo' lad". The outfit came out of the channel, with everything dripping wet.

Catching shrimps is an occupation from March until the onset of the first frosts. "I can almost guarantee to get a few shrimps about the 20th of March," says Jack Manning. Shrimps leave Morecambe Bay as the water temperature falls in autumn, "though they can still be caught off the

Left: **A tractor that had become mired in Holy Well Dyke.** *Above:* **Sorting shrimps.**

edge of the sea at Blackpool and down off the Mersey." The size and quality of Morecambe Bay shrimps has declined. It is not likely to be the consequence of over-fishing, because it is reckoned that the fishermen of Flookburgh work only about a quarter of the whole area available to the shrimps. "We certainly don't scrape it all." Shrimping consists of driving tractor and trailer into a channel and towing a trawl. As the bar on the trawl is dragged along the sand, there is an upsurge of water, and "whatever is there" is swept up over the bar and into the net." In the days of horses and carts, night-time was the main period for fishing. Jack Manning recalls when he had two horses and, in the boom years, was going out on both tides. Four or five years ago, night-fishing for shrimps became unrewarding. He cannot explain the absence of shrimps from the net at grounds where a fisherman might go by day and do well. (Night-fishing for shrimps is still possible, though, off Morecambe). The price of shrimps has kept pace with inflation rather better than the price of some other products. Catching them is therefore a worth-while occupation. Yet there are now few shrimps to catch. Some believe that an important reason for the depletion of the stock is pollution of the habitat.

Flookburgh, like Morecambe, has a fisherman's co-operative, handling the catches. Shrimps are packed into cartons and covered with a layer of warm butter before the lid is attached. The main shrimp season is from the latter part of August through to December. The special character of the Flookburgh shrimps is derived from the fact that they are boiled in fresh, not sea water. In the old days, "picking" shrimps occupied a large number of womenfolk around the Bay. Two old ladies at Morecambe "picked" 1,128,000 shrimps in 12 months. At Flookburgh, one lady started with 13lb. of "shrimps in the shell", enough to fill two good buckets, and within an hour she had produced 3¼lb. of "shrimp meat". The feat was possible because they were large shrimp, in good condition. A good picker produces from 1½lb. to 2lb. of picked shrimps an hour.

Reference has already been made to the cast-iron boiler in the outhouse where shrimps are boiled. The wives contrived to have the water on the boil as soon as the menfolk arrived home. "You always gave the missus a good idea of what time you would be home; if it was warm,

'clashy' weather the sooner the shrimps were boiled the better. If they were a bit on the dead side, they were never good to pick." The shrimps were boiled up several times. If one or two were tested, and found to be a bit on the "tuggy" side, they would be left "on the boil" a little longer.

Before laws relating to hygiene were introduced, boiled shrimps were spread on the ground on hessian sacking, the hessian soaking up the water. "It's illegal now. You have to have trays, well above the ground." The shrimps were once scalded, for cleanliness, after they had been "picked". It made a shrimp look better, though it didn't have the same good flavour! The shrimp-pickers of Flookburgh were a gregarious lot, laughing, chattering and gossiping the hours away. "It's difficult to get people to do it now. They say they don't want to bother!"

The fluke, or flounder, has a white belly, with brown on the topside. The tone can vary, depending on the nature of the sea bed where it rests. "I've had a lot of flukes in my time. We used to catch a hundredweight, head 'em and fillet 'em and leave 'em on the bone. They were in the best condition if caught in September. Dad didn't have a deep-freeze or owt like that; when he caught 'em they had to go. He'd sell his flukes from the house or down on the shore. Through the war, they were bagged up and sent by rail to Manchester." Flukes are caught in nets attached to stakes and left out for a tide. "The knack lies in being out there as soon as possible, before the gulls!" Sometimes, if the nets were set on a high bank in wild weather, the stakes would be pounded by the waves and brought to the surface. "You'd go after a blow and find your nets had gone, or they'd lifted and become tangled."

Fluke disappear when the hard frost comes. "It's got to be hard frost, not just a touch of frost. They go, in any case, about the beginning of February, when they spawn. If the hard frost comes in December, they will disappear then, and we won't see them again till they come back in about April. There's a meal in one good fluke, for it weighs about a pound. "We fillet flukes now. It's only come in during the past 20 years. Before that, flukes were sold complete. Old Tom Wilson started to sell filleted flukes from a basket, which he carried on his arm. He went round the villages . . ." They are difficult fish to sell. The housewife expects her fish packaged and breaded and just ready for the pan. "Years

ago, people used to smoke fluke by hanging them in the chimney of the house. That wouldn't go down well now." The price received for fluke is "hopeless", we should record. They are selling, wholesale, at only twice the price they attained in 1942.

Above: ***A group taken on Silverdale foreshore. In the picture are Flookburgh men and women who had travelled to Silverdale to collect cockles. Notice the thick clothing (modern, lightweight waterproofs were to be a boon to fisher-folk) and also the leggings and clogs. (Photograph reproduced by Peter Cherry from an old print).***

Life at Holker

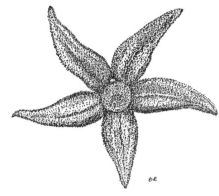

STARFISH

AS TRAINS clatter across the viaduct at the Leven near Holker, it is appropriate to reflect that it was the Cavendish family of Holker who played an important part in establishing the railway that by its substantial embankments fixed the position of much of the shore. A railway embankment takes the swagger from the tides. The Cavendish family, already much involved in estate management and industry (notably the slate quarries of Furness) had five other country seats but appear to have been especially fond of Holker (pronounced Hooker), situated between a range of wooded hills, where buzzards circle and call, and the bird-busy shoreline of the Leven estuary. Their railway connection began with the Earl of Burlington, who visited Holker periodically until, in 1840. A very happy marriage ended with the sudden death of his wife, leaving the Earl distraught. The grieving widower retired to Holker. He was occupying himself with local matters when railway proposals were being made. He supported the scheme and, by that support, encouraged other landowners to take part. (The Earl became the seventh Duke of Devonshire in 1858. He was known to local folk as "the old Duke").

The verdant appearance of Holker belies its situation. The name is said to mean "hollow marsh". The estate in Furness is in three parts and in the Cartmel area, there are about 11,000 acres, comprising the Leven Estuary, the land along its shores and to the east on either side of Cartmel, together with a small area in the Winster valley. South of

*Left: **Areas of Morecambe Bay dried out sufficiently for this early type of sand-yacht to be used. The photograph was taken by the Leven. Right — Top, left: Lord Richard Cavendish and Lady Moira Cavendish, with a group pictured beside Morecambe Bay in Edwardian times.** Top right: **Winston Churchill in a group paddling in the river Leven, where they appeared to be building a dam. Churchill's mother, Clementine, was a regular visitor to Holker Hall.** Bottom: **Lord Salisbury pushing off a punt occupied by Lord Sidney Herbert at the mouth of the Leven in 1919.***

Right: Gardeners at Holker Hall at the turn of the century. The same extensive acreage of garden is now maintained by only four men.

Left: Members of the Cavendish family enjoyed days spent cockling, with traditional horse and cart, on the sands of Morecambe Bay. This picture dates from 1932.

Mereness Point (alternative spelling, Meanness and Mearness) are the wooded cliffs of Roudsea Wood and off-shore Herring Rocks followed by a series of limestone cliffs, each with its former lime-kiln. These are Skelwith, Little Arrad, Reake and Ravensbarrow.

Park Head was a former loading jetty. Prior to the formation of sea embankments and the construction of the railway, the headlands were the only definite features in a semi-tidal marsh. Further south and east there is the headland at Quarry Flat, much of which was quarried for the construction of Cartmel Priory. The other headlands, at Humphrey Head and Kirk Head, are well-known.

Miss A.M. Wakefield wrote in 1909 about the celebrated Holker Mosses, of approximately 600 acres. The Westmorland vocalist, who inaugurated a famous musical festival, loved the shores of Morecambe Bay and noted of the area of the Mosses: "It is quite undisturbed, though a highway runs along its edge, but on the mosses themselves the birds and the peat-cutters have a monopoly of sound among the tracts of lily of the valley and the beds of the wild andromeda." Fringes cut for peat have now been colonised by alder. Elsewhere there is natural regeneration of Scots pine, birch and some oak.

The mansion of today is largely a Victorian building, constructed following the gutting of an earlier building by fire in 1871. Some of the old Hall remains in view. The Cavendish family has been linked with Holker since 1756, prior to which the Prestons lived here; the two families had links through marriage.

A photograph in this book gives an indication of the size of the gardening staff in the latter days of "the old Duke". So many gardeners worked here that now and again they were able to field a cricket team against a team representing the gardening staff of one of the other dukal homes, Chatsworth in Derbyshire.

Holker Hall and Park are "open to view" in the tourist season and the Lakeland Rose Show is held here.

*Right: **An Edwardian "jape" with donkey and cart near Holker Hall.***

Leven and Chapel Isle

ON THE SKEERS

ALFRED BUTLER is the Guide over Leven Estuary and the Leven carries the overflow from Windermere, England's largest lake. Mr. Butler holds his office as Guide under the Duchy of Lancaster (which is the case with Cedric, as Guide over Kent Sands). When he is at home, Mr. Butler has an enviable view. He can scan an area of the Leven from the railway viaduct to wooded Chapel Island, where — so they say — monks were on prayerful vigil as people crossed the Bay at low tide. Beyond the estuary are marsh and meadow, culminating in wooded fells.

Alfred Butler has presided over the estuarial Leven for almost 40 years; he is also an industrious fisherman. He grew up at Allithwaite, where his father, Jonathan, his grandfather Robert and umpteen generations of Butlers made their living collecting flukes, shrimps, cockles and mussels. Ask Alfred Butler to explain about the working of the tide, how the sands shift and how it is vital to find a bar that gives a firm crossing of the estuary, and he smiles the smile of one who does it naturally, his mind working at computer speed, arriving at a reliable assessment of the situation without recourse to paper, pencil and book, which is the case with almost all the fishermen around Morecambe Bay.

His house, some 10 yards from the shore, has four times been flooded by the sea. "Strong winds and a lot of rain make the biggest tides," he says. Some work has been done on the sea wall to cheat all but the highest tides. He points to sections of the wall and to the end of the pier — an old pier, near the foot of the former Ulverston canal — where stones weighing from five to six hundredweights have been moved by the fiercest tides. These mainly arrive in autumn and winter.

As a Guide, Alfred Butler is always interesting, with his tales of how porpoise have been seen in the river and with recollections of the good old days when it was not very difficult to catch a salmon. Now there are relatively few fish to be found. Alfred is one of the men licensed to operate a lave-net, and with it he has caught salmon up to 26lb. in weight. "You can't make a living out of catching salmon now. I hardly bother with them," he says.

As a fisherman, he goes to the Bay in the traditional way — on wheels. His tractor and trailer cover seven or eight miles to the places where he can trawl for shrimps. These are boiled, then "picked" by local women, including his wife. The picked shrimps are frozen for later delivery to a firm in Annan, north of Solway. (For some years, he was able to dispose of them at the factory in Cark). Flukes are disposed of locally. Alfred Butler has a good cockle bed, where he operates — in time-honoured way — with a Jumbo, the wooden implement that is used to agitate the sands and bring up the shellfish. Cockles are boiled, then frozen for later delivery to towns in West Yorkshire. The cockles are sold in their shells in winter, when the keeping quality is much improved.

The Jumbo was invented almost a century ago by a man called Peter Butler, of Flookburgh, who accidentally came across the principle. His implement, which revolutionised the cockle industry of the Bay, comprises a base board four feet six inches long, 14 inches wide and about half an inch

Alfred Butler is the Guide to the Leven Sands. He has also been an industrious fisherman in Morecambe Bay for many years. He is pictured (right) with cockles and flukes. Mr. Butler's home is at Canal Foot, Ulverston.

Left: Cockles. These three-year-old specimens were collected from clean sand in Morecambe Bay and are of the very best quality. In collecting cockles, the Bay fisherman uses a three-pronged implement known as a "craam".

thick; four uprights of lighter wood, and two handles. The operator simply grips the handles and wobbles the implement, the base board setting up a stir in the sand — and up come the cockles, to be collected by a *craam,* or three-pronged fork, or in some good seasons by a rake! They will tell you, along the coast, that to use the Jumbo you need suction and you need water. "If there is a drying wind, you go to the cockle beds as soon as you can. If you get a windy day, and it is blowing hard, the sand dries out pretty quickly and you'll have to come home sooner than you planned because you cannot work properly."

There are plenty of cockles, but the price paid for them is not good. Early this century, up to 10 railway wagon loads of cockles at a time left the station at Cark, and in the 19th century — before the railway was constructed — cockles caught on the sandbanks below Flookburgh were carted to Hest Bank for despatch to Preston by canal boat. (At that time, incidentally, the Bay was open for boats and 24 craft were kept at Flookburgh and used for cockling). In the late 1940s, a scarcity of cockles to the north of Morecambe Bay led William Robinson (Cedric's father) and Jim Benson to seek new grounds near Silverdale, to which they arranged to travel by train. Good beds were found and so they returned with horses and carts to exploit them, staying overnight to avoid wasting too much time in travel. The two men knew the local fishermen, but later — as they worked the cockle beds near Bolton-le-Sands and at Hest Bank — there was some opposition from men they had not previously met. "One of them thought he owned the grounds. He very nearly did, because he was a big, strapping man!" William Robinson recalls a man who cycled to Hest Bank from Morecambe with a Jumbo on his bike. Another cockle fisherman had a fruit and fish round in Lancaster.

Jack Manning talks of the ups and downs of the cockling trade. Some of the men who retailed cockles were "odd bag men", going round the streets with horses and carts, selling cockles along with a variety of other produce. Some dealers who did not live in the immediate area were "rumlads". They handled cockles on commission. Walter Benson recalls: "In the 1920s, my Uncle Eddie asked Dad if there was a chance of a week's cockling, for times were bad. Dad said: 'Well, we can give it a go. I haven't a lot of faith, but

Above: **A disused quay at Greenodd, near Ulverston, as it was in August, 1957. The quay was constructed at the junction of the rivers Crake and Leven.**

we'll try it for a week.' So they tried it for a week; they worked hard and sent their cockles away on commission. Eddie came across on the Saturday morning at the time fishermen were opening their letters, anticipating postal orders, and he said: 'How have we done?' Dad had reckoned it up and replied: 'If you give me 1s.8d. we'll be about straight!' That was just the thing to reduce a fellow, wasn't it?"

Alfred Butler, operating from Canal Foot at Ulverston, has memories of Flookburgh in the days when wagon loads of cockles left the local station daily during the season. He remembers when up to 20 horses and carts were operating from this little village and when running costs were low. "It now costs you more to go shrimping — diesel fuel isn't cheap — than what was paid to a man as a week's wage in those days." Out on the sands, he is often in the company of Leslie Salisbury, for it is unwise for a man to operate alone in case the tractor engine fails. Alfred Butler once had the experience of rowing a boat with a tractor in tow! His tractor had become bogged down. "It took two days to get it out of the sand, and we fastened a dozen 40-gallon drums to her for buoyancy. We tried to pull her with a long rope, but the rope kept snagging. So I went for my rowing boat — and rowed the tractor back to the shore at Newbiggin." Truly a novel sight.

With regard to mussels, the Morecambe Bay fishermen used to visit the hard skeers. "In the old days," a Flookburgh man relates, "people ate 'em and enjoyed 'em. You can take them even yet for your own use. Some of these East Coast fishermen like 'em for bait." There was a time when up to 20 boats, anchored at Sandgate, went out with the tide and down to Piel, collecting mussels with "big, long-shafted drags." Tragedy befell one family. "The fishermen had loaded up the boats and were on their way back on some wild, rough water when it was decided to anchor for a while before crossing the most exposed area. The Robinson lads decided to continue. They had a lot o' mussels in the boat, which got to bumping and banging. The boat sank, and the lads were drowned."

Anyone who visits Hammerside, beside the Leven, where Mr. Butler's home can be found, becomes aware of Glaxo, the industrial giant that uses the old Ulverston Canal as a static water tank. The canal, sealed off from the sea, was once known as the shortest canal in the land. Almost two centuries ago, it added prosperity to "Bonnie Lile Ooston". On the day when the canal was opened — a chilly day in December, 1796 — the folk of Ulverston streamed from their homes to observe the arrival of the first craft from the Bay. Ships were lined up, ready to sail to the town. The brig *Sally,* from London, decked with colours, was the first to enter. The sloop *Content* delivered a load of coal.

The broad canal carried a whiff of the sea up to Ulverston town, where ship-building once flourished and the streets of Ulverston were thronged by ship's captains, carpenters, caulkers and craftsmen of marine architecture. When, in 1944, the railway company decided to close the canal — then greatly in need of cleaning and dredging, not forgetting repairs to the lock gates — a local writer declared: "On the whole it seems that the canal, the picturesque apanage of 'bonnie lile Ooston', will have to go the way of all romantic and derelict anachronisms."

A Common Bird in Morecambe Bay

WHEREVER YOU GO around Morecambe Bay, you will observe the oystercatcher, a dandy of the shoreline, with handsome pied plumage, a bill that is long and red — like a stick of sealing wax — and flesh-pink legs. This bird has a shrill piping call. When a number of birds are calling together, the sound can be deafening. At nesting time, the oyster-catcher pair make a shallow scrape on shingle, sometimes lining it with shells. The large eggs have a cryptic colouration. At other times of the year, tens of thousands of oystercatchers throng the sky above the bay or form dense, dark patches on the beach as the birds take their rest. Fishermen have no great love for the oystercatcher, accusing it of taking far too many shellfish. That large red bill can be used most deftly to open a cockle or a smaller shellfish called locally a "henpenny".

Islands of the Bay

GREYLAG GOOSE

THE CLUSTER of islands off the Furness coast give a touch of romance to Morecambe Bay, though Walney, Roa and Foulney are tethered to the mainland. Only Piel, with ruins that have a theatrical flavour, remains free. The "island" of Roa looks like a small suburb that became marooned in the Bay. It is connected to Rampside by a causeway (known locally as the Embankment or Banking). A local hotel, the strangely-named *Concle,* is supposedly derived from "Conc Hole", a deep place where ships once lay at anchor. We have found no written confirmation of this story. Roa, a Scandinavian name anciently rendered Ro-ey, has 36 houses and a population of about 100. It has always been of a modest size, and a 16th century writer referred to this and the island of Foulney as "plots of no great compasse".

Roa has slithered economically from being a bustling place, to which trains ran, and from which steamers sailed, to the status of an "island" where the people seek work elsewhere, notably in the workshops of Barrow. (Incidentally, the train service ended in 1936). The thick walls of the old customs house are faced with sea pebbles. During the 1939–45 war, a land-mine dropped nearby, and the fabric was so shaken that about 20 feet of its height was removed for safety. Trinity Terrace on Roa Island was constructed to provide accommodation for the pilots when 10 Trinity House men resided here. The pilot cutter is moored at Barrow. From the tip of Roa, one can enjoy the spectacle of quite large ships passing close by, for the Walney channel lies between Piel and Roa.

There is usually a breeze blowing on Roa and, as at Barrow, you can always recognise a local man because he grasps his hat as he approaches a corner! The spring tide rises up to 32 feet, with the peak of the neap tides running at about 14 feet. The "big house" was built for H.W. Schneider, an industrialist, and though a wing of the red brick building was demolished, 20 rooms remain. A row of seven cannon points seawards. There is a story that Schneider acquired the cannon so that a salute could be fired as a yacht carrying foreign Royalty passed Roa. Again, we have not confirmed the story, but it is true to Schneider's nature.

Foulney Island extends from the Roa causeway. It lost its island status in Victorian times when, a causeway having been built to Roa, it was decided to build an embankment from it to Foulney to curb the ebb tide, which on sweeping round by Ulverston had deposited silt in a channel being used by boats. To state that Foulney is 28 acres in extent is simply to quote from the books. A fierce tide, over-running part of Foulney, can carry away a mass of material and heap it up not far away. The island is forever changing its size and shape. The flow tide litters the beaches of Foulney with rubbish, including heaps of mussel shells. So dense are the mussel beds that parts of the Bay are blackened with them, and the area can support an imposing number of eiders, the podgy sea-going ducks. Several hundred eiders nest on Walney and a few pairs prospect for nests on Foulney. Fishermen, who are the most frequent visitors to Foulney throughout the year, gather baulks of wood to make themselves shelters against the wind. They also make impressive beach fires. Blue as well as red flames run along the heaps of salt-impregnated wood. The island provides places where anglers can stand while fishing for sea bass.

56

Architecture on Roa Island, which is now connected by a causeway to the mainland. From Roa extends a pebbly strand known as Foulney Island. The imposing house (left) was the home of one of the successful Furness industrialists.

Foulney is said to have been known as Fowle Island, referring to the abundance of nesting sea birds. A 16th century document relating to the revenues of Furness Abbey mentions that on Foulney bred "innumerable fowle of dyvers kyndes upon the erth emongs the grasse and stones, for there ys neither tree nor bushe growinge there." Much has changed around Morecambe Bay, but Foulney retains its appeal to sea birds, especially the delightful "sea swallows" (terns). Their flickering wings, seen against the blue of a springtime sky and backlit, appear to be transparent. Five species of tern nest on the shingle spit extending from Foulney, and a succession of wardens has watched over the birds during the nesting season. The tides provide a never-ending worry. Periodically, the shingle spit goes under water and tern eggs or chicks are swept away.

The island's rich and varied flora conceals the nests of oystercatcher, ringed plover, some eider ducks, red-breasted merganser, redshank and meadow pipit. Foulney is a remarkable grandstand from which to view wintering birds — waders and ducks. (It was on nearby Piel, according to the *Herball* of a well-known 16th century naturalist, Gerard, that the barnacle goose was bred out of barnacles!).

John Moore used to operate across the channel between Roa and Piel, where the water is very exposed, and often lashed into foam by the wind. There is a 20 feet rise and fall of water. Mr. Moore used to relate that pilots living on Piel Island helped the wooden ships to make their landings. "Those were the days of wooden ships and iron men," he would say. Dan Rooney, the King of Piel Island would be waiting for visitors to Piel Island. John Moore tied up, then led the way to the *Ship Inn,* where Mr. Rooney presided.

If there was a reasonable number of people on Piel Island, a visitor might be made a Knight of the Ancient Order of Piel Castle. The penalty consisted of paying for drinks for all in the bar. The landlord or an existing Knight could perform the ceremony. If a woman was concerned, she became a Baroness. The members of this Order must conform to certain rules. They must be of good behaviour, steady and at all times attentive to the opposite sex. They had to see to the welfare of all visitors to the Island during their stay, "and if it should happen that there are any sports taking place on the island, such as boat-racing, cock-fighting, bull-baiting or pigeon-shooting, then it is your duty to help the King with your assistance in any way that your service may be required."

The charge continued: "Finally, let it be impressed on your mind that you must be a free drinker, a moderate smoker and, an ardent lover of the opposite sex." If it should ever fall to a Knight's unfortunate lot to be wrecked and drowned on Piel Island, he was at liberty to go to the hotel and demand a free night's lodging, "and as much as you can eat or drink!"

South Walney is best-known for its gullery. There is a community of herring and lesser black-backed gulls, totalling some 60,000 pairs. Gulls can be heard calling by day and night, from their return to the nesting grounds early in the year to their dispersal with the surviving young towards the end of August and into September. During the winter, Walney cleanses itself, the winter gales and periods of hard frost helping to obliterate the debris of a huge bird city.

Walney is tethered to Barrow by a bridge, at either end of which are traffic lights. Vickerstown, the main settlement, is mainly a dormitory for Barrow. Some of the spirit of Old Walney is detectable at Biggar, a hamlet raised a little from the low ground. The visitor to South Walney passes near the Barrow tip, which is patronised by gulls, some of which have been seen flying away with tins attached to their webbed feet! Walney, a natural breakwater for Barrow, has been greatly battered down the years. In November 1977, for example, a westerly gale which demolished the pier at Morecambe tore from the west shore of Walney a strip of land 30 feet deep; the main track down the island from the former coastguard cottages to the lighthouse was breached in two places.

The shingle beaches of Walney slope up gradually from the sea's edge to where grasses and assorted flowers have rooted. Here, in June, are to be seen the spires of vipers bugloss. The island is decked by yellow sandwort and pink campion, and you may have the pleasure of being shown a clump of the unattractive but glamorous oyster plant. Walney is long and slender, curving in at the ends as though to give special protection to Barrow. In size and shape it is comparable with Windermere. The highest

Below: **John Moore, the former ferryman between Roa and Piel islands. He used to relate that pilots lived on Piel Island "in the days of wooden ships and iron men."**

Above: **Dan Rooney and his wife on Piel Island about a quarter of a century ago. Dan, the "King" of Piel Island, presided over the inn there. He used to initiate male visitors into the Ancient Order of Piel Castle. The remains of that castle are seen in our picture.**

point, Beacon Hill, is a modest 78 feet above sea level. Just off Walney lies Morecambe Bay's most insignificant island — Sheep Island — where, it is said, sailors with infectious diseases were isolated.

South Walney has topographical variety: dunes thatched with marram, expanses of shore grass and bracken, minor canyons lined with shingle and sand, lagoons of various sizes (some of fresh water, others flavoured with salt) heaps of gravel and even a battered pier from which boats once took building materials to the up-and-coming Lancaster resorts. A lighthouse sticks up near a muddy bay.

One of our special friends, Walter Shepherd, was for years the warden of this bird reserve. Walter wore a trilby, and if it appeared to have been white-washed, the time of the hatching of the gull eggs had arrived! Adult birds are especially pugnacious at that time, diving on intruders. From sea-watching hides set up near the main channel, ornithologists scan the winter tides, which bring in such fascinating birds as merganser and scoter. Tens of thousands of oystercatchers may congregate in the area of the hides at the highest tides. About 500 northern golden plover inhabit a tract of damp pastureland north of the reserve throughout the winter. Some "windfalls" of migrating birds are spectacular. One stormy spring day about 40,000 knot, showing "breeding red", arrived and rested for half a day on the beaches of this low pebble-and-sand island.

*Left: **The skeletal forms of cranes at the Barrow shipyard where, today, nuclear-powered submarines are among the craft made. The photograph was taken from the shore on Walney Island.** Right: **Arnside Auxiliary Coastguards muster to receive the thanks of those they have saved from the sea.***

Life of a Sands Guide

AS A FISHERMAN and Guide to the Sands, Cedric has taken part in the making of several television documentary films. The first was in 1974, when he co-operated with Bob Langley, who is well-known for his appearances on the BBC programme *Pebble Mill at One*. Cedric's role was to be on horseback, leading a coach and pair across the Sands, with Bob as a passenger in the coach. Not having ridden for a number of years, Cedric chose one of his quietest ponies — the old and faithful Shyan — which seemed determined to do everything wrong. Shyan moved fast when he should have gone slowly; he continually turned his head away from the camera to eat the laurels which Cedric had slung over his shoulders, intent on using them as "brobs" to mark out the route. Yet when the whole film, *A Lakeland Summer,* was projected, it was counted as a success.

In October of the following year, Granada Television filmed Cedric and his son, Paul, as they fished for whitebait. The film included sequences showing the family at Guides Farm as they processed the catch and packed it for the market. The producer of this film was Peter Carr, and it was called *Sand Pilot*. (Peter was to become a friend of the Robinson family, and he still visits the Farm).

BBC Television's *Blue Peter* filmed Cedric on the Sands five years later. Simon Groom was accompanied by his famous retriever, "Goldie" (Jean, Cedric's daughter, and "Goldie" adopted each other for the two days of filming). Sequences were filmed at the cockle beds and fluke nets. In 1982, Thames Television used the theme of the Guide and the Bay for an educational film, *The Sandman,* which included filming at some quicksands and also a "take" of a school party splashing through the river Kent. On the last day, the film crew watched and filmed at close quarters the famous Morecambe Bay "bore" as it raced in, heralding the tide. Back at Guides Farm, Cedric invited two Flookburgh

CEDRIC ROBINSON

fishermen — Brian Shaw and Harold Benson — to be interviewed by the producer, Peter Tabern.

Cedric has appeared in a programme in the *Down to Earth* series (Granada Television). Bob Smithies met and interviewed Cedric in the unfamiliar setting of large television studios at Manchester. Later Cedric commented: "I felt so relaxed in his company, apart from feeling like a baked potato under the lights!" In the summer of 1980, Alisdair McDonald, of the BBC, and a cameraman, walked across the Bay with Cedric to film a typical guided walk. It began on the foreshore of Morecambe Lodge Farm, Bolton-le-Sands, and there was a halt at Jenny Brown's Point for a short break. Then it was "off" once again, over the Sands towards Grange.

In the spring of 1981, Cedric met the well-known historian, A.J.P. Taylor, when he was preparing a film about a Lancashire journey, under the title *Edge of Britain*.

Above: **The lighthouse at the southern tip of Walney Island, off Barrow-in-Furness. The buildings are virtually surrounded by nesting birds — mainly gulls and terns.** *Right:* **A Walney oyster-catcher leaves its nest on a pebble beach on South Walney. A handsome pied bird, with a bright red bill, it is known as "sea pie" in the locality.**

Left: A huge mussel bed near Roa Island. Above: One of the many local eiders at its nest on Walney. The local abundance of eider is related to the huge quantities of shellfish in this part of Morecambe Bay.

A great black-backed gull about to incubate its eggs on Walney Island.

There was a stiff south-westerly wind, and in due course much of the filming took place in the lee of Humphrey Head. In April, 1983, a group of children from Allithwaite School, with teachers and parents, volunteered to take part in a short film prepared by Tyne Tees Television for a series of children's programmes called "Madabout". Mathew Kelly was the TV personality involved; he distributed signed photographs of himself to the children, and a party of those involved was entertained to tea at Abbot Hall, Kents Bank.

Judith Chalmers was filmed on the Bay in the summer of 1984 for an item in the holiday programme *Wish You Were Here*. Judith told Cedric that the Cross Bay walk was the highlight of her visit; never before had she had an experience quite like that!

The most ambitious of the Morecambe Bay films was that "shot" by Yorkshire Television and entitled *Men of the Wet Sahara*. It was prepared as part of a series of documentaries called "Once in a Lifetime". Superb shots by the cameraman, Moustafa Hamouri, of silhouettes against one of Morecambe Bay's best sunsets captured the beauty of it all. This one-hour film took 18 months to film. During this time, the director and his two researchers, Kathy Rooney and Julie O'Hare, were frequently in touch with Guides Farm. Cedric kept them informed about the weather, tide-times and the type of fishing being undertaken.

Many sequences were taken from a helicopter, and when aerial photography began there was an almighty "bang" and £200,000 of helicopter — also the pilot and cameraman — dropped out of the sky, fortunately without inflicting serious injuries on the two men. Meanwhile, the tractors continued to race across the Sands, their drivers not realising that anything had happened. Those fishermen had been told not to look up at the cameras while they were being filmed! (The cause of the accident remains a mystery).

It was an experience for Cedric, and the other fishermen, to contribute to the making of this fine documentary — though, says Cedric, "I would be telling a lie if I said I enjoyed it. The most enjoyable time came later, when filming was over and our friends, Derrick and Decima Cooper, Brian Shaw, his wife Laura and their son Dean — along with Olive and myself — were invited to the studios of Yorkshire Television in Leeds·for a preview of the film . . . Dean remembers in particular sitting in the canteen with the cast of *Emmerdale Farm* not far away!"

Dear Mr. Robinson . . .

Letters from schoolchildren

Thank you for the tractor ride, out seven miles into the bay. I have learnt a lot about fishing, and thank you for letting us gather lots of cockles. When I got home I washed my cockles, and then let them soak until they opened, then next day we had cockles for dinner.

— Sandy Fowler

Thank you for taking me down onto the sands. I enjoyed it very much. You showed me many interesting things. I often got splattered by the jumbo board. I was the only one in the family that liked cockles. I had a lovely time.

— Rose Townley

Thank you for taking us across the sands and for showing us lots of nice and interesting things. We saw crabs and sand in worm shapes. It was really good. I liked going to the cockle beds and I gathered a lot of them. I enjoyed racing the tractor on the way back. You won us twice but the third time we won you by a mile.

— Peter Whittaker

Thank you for taking us on your tractor and trailer. It was good fun. The best bit was when we had our dinner. I was at the front with Mr. Worthington. Thank you for your extra time.

— Matthew Smyth

Mathew Kelly, a television personality, with a group from Allithwaite School.

You made a very interesting talk about the bay. I used to come and ride your horses when I was a bit younger. I think it was very good when you talked about quicksands. Now we will all know.

— Carole Perie

Thank you for coming to the school and telling us about the bay and telling us about the dangers, and about the stories about people sinking. I enjoyed it very much.

— Iain Richardson

Thank you for a lovely talk. Thank you for giving up your time to come and talk to us. I know we all thoroughly enjoyed it. I thought the bit about the boy on the motor bike was interesting. I enjoyed watching the Duke crossing the sands.

— Sarah Tomlinson

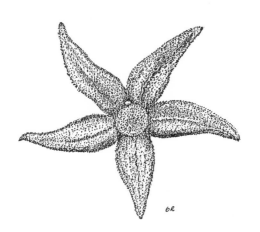

I hope you and Domino, Shyan, Ladybird, Sparkie, Minstrel, Bluey, Danny, Flash, Tinkerbell, Dougal and Dillan are well. Not forgetting Mrs. Robinson and Jean and Chris. Thank you for coming and talking to us about the bay. I'm sure we all enjoyed it. Thank you for answering all our questions. You have been a great help. I hope to be coming down to see the horses in the summer holidays.

— Claire Davenport
(The one who helps with the horses).

Thank you for a very interesting morning. I thought it was good about the quicksand, crossing the bay I've been across on the bay and when we were going through a channel I had to pull my friend through. I like it when you talked about fishing on Morecambe Bay. It would be nice if they still sold cockles from Morecambe Bay. You did very well in taking the Duke across the bay.

— Laura Nolan

Thank you for your talk about the bay and your time today. I enjoyed the talk because the things you said were useful to know, because I live near the bay I saw you and the Duke at Kents Bank Station, and all the other horses and carts following you.

— Stephanie Palmer

Thank you for coming to school to talk to us about the bay. I couldn't come and watch the Duke of Edinburgh because I was away but I saw it in the paper. I think that the best things on Cross bay walks are the deep waters because you can swim in them, and the Cows bellies (wobbly sinking sand) because we can jump on them without sinking. I have been on several cross bay walks I went from Silvedale back to Kents Bank which was last year and I went on one from Grange to Arnside then back on the train.

— Joanne Coles
P.S. I like walking on the sands in bare feet because the shrimps tickle my feet.

Morecambe Bay Dialect

THE TRUE Morecambe Bay dialect can now only be found in use by fishermen, and this is rapidly dying out. The only reason for its survival is that many of the words used by the fishermen have no modern equivalent. The following glossary has been prepared by Keith Willacy:

A.S.: Anglo Saxon
O.N.: Old Norse

Aan = to own. A.S. Agan. to own.
Afoor = before. A.S. f'or.
Aither = either. A.S. aegfer (p'th).
Asc = to ask. A.S. acsian, ascian.
Bauk, balk, bawk = Piece of timber or a fishing baulk. A.S. balca, also a long wattled hedge. Old Norse = a hedge of wood.
Barfet = barefoot. A.S. barfot. O.N. berfoettr.
Beäl = to shout, roar or bellow. O.N. belja.
Beck = a stream or brook. O.N. beckr or bekkr.
Bedding = bedclothes. A.S. bedding.
Blaan = out of breath. A.S. blawan (to blow hard).
Boose = cattle stall. A.S. bosg.
Brid = a bird. A.S. brid.
Brock = a badger. A.S. broc.
Cant = to raise one end. O.N. kanta.
Carr = a swampy field. O.N. kjor.
Chap = a general term for a man. O.N. kjaft.
Clout = a heavy blow. A.S. clūt.
Corf = a basket used by fishermen. O.N. karfa.
Cote = a house or cottage. A.S. cōte.
Creefer = a louse. A.S crewfere.
Crinkle = a shuffling. O.N. kringil.
Daan = dawn. O.N. dagan.
Delve = to dig. A.S. delfan.
Dem = to stop water, dam. A.S. dimman.
Dike = to make a fence or ditch. A.S. diftan. Noun diki.
Diker = a hedger or ditcher. A.S. dicere.

Dikin = the act of ditching. A.S. dicung.
Ding = to throw violently. O.N. dingia.
Draff = malt after brewing, used for cattle feed. A.S. drabble. O.N. draf.
Ea = water generally. A river channel. The river Kent as it runs down the Lancaster sands. Morecambe Bay is called "The Ea". A.S. Ea. The river beck at Cark in Cartmel has always been called The Ea, and still is to this day.
Earand = an errand. O.N. erende. A.S. oërend.
Eaw = a ewe. A.S. eaw.
Efter = after. A.S. and O.N. efter.
Eyok = an oak. A.S. ac, oec. O.N. eyk.
Fell = to knock down. A.S. fellan.
Foor = a furrow. A.S. furk.
Ga or *Gaa* = to go. O.N. ga.
Garth = an enclosure. A.S. gearel. O.N. gardr.
Ginnel or *gannel* = a channel. A.S. ganol.
Ginners = gills of a fish. A.S. and O.N. ginian.
Glister = to sparkle. O.N. gloëstr.
Gowk = a fool. A.S. geac. O.N. gaufr.
Greet = to weep. O.N. greta. A.S. groetan.
Handsel = first money for sale of goods. A.S. landselen. O.N. landsal.
Heft = haft or handle. A.S. hoëft.
Hesp = a hasp to fasten a door. A.S. hoefsian. O.N. hesfa.
Hide = to beat or flog. O.N. Hȳda.
Holm = an island (Holm Island) or low-lying land often surrounded by water, or swamp (Anstable Holm). O.N. holm, holmi.
Hull = a shed, cow shed, pig hull, calf hull, a cabin. A.S. hule.
Ing = a marshy meadow. A.S. ing. O.N. eng.
Jannock = upright, straighforward. O.N. jafn.
Kewin = a periwinkle. O.N. knyta.
Lake = to play. A.S. lāc. O.N. leikr.
Leck = a leak. O.N. leki.
Len = to lend. A.S. Lōēnan.

Left: **Judith Chalmers, a television personality, with Simon Ward, photographed as she prepared a holiday programme on Morecambe Bay in 1984.** *Above:* **Melvyn Bragg on the Sands in the spring of 1985.**

Lig = to lie down.   O.N. leggji.
Loll = to loiter.   O.N. lolla.
Lound = dead calm.   O.N. logn.
Mell = a mallet, wooden hammer, a two handled hammer. O.N. melia.
Melr = a sand dune.
Neaf = the fish.   O.N. knefi.
Neb = the nose. Small cockles.   A.S. neb.   O.N. nebbi.
Narsh = nearest.   O.N. noerst.
Neese = to sneeze.   A.S. niesan.   O.N. knjosa.
Parrock = a small field.   A.S. farnec.   O.N. fearroc.
Reek = smoke, smell. fumes.   A.S. reyht.   O.N. roēc.
Rimmer = name. Rim of mere.
Rive = to tear.   O.N. rifa.
Roggle = to shake.   O.N. rugl.
Sea tangle = seaweed.   O.N. vaungull.
Shard = shallow.
Slape = slippery, level sand, where fast-running tide smooths the surface.   O.N. slaefr.
Span = new, quite new.   O.N. spān nӯr.
Stick knife = pocket knife.   O.N. sticknifr.
Stirk = a year old beast.   A.S. stirc.
Teem = to pour out.   O.N. tōēma.
Thrang = busy.   A.S. vrang.   O.N. vraungr (pro., v as th).
Threaten = A.S. vreatian.
Throstle = A.S. vrosle.
Torf = turf.   O.N. torf.
Thole pin = peg for oars.   O.N. volk.
Trunnel = wheel of a wheelbarrow.   A.S. trendel.
Tul = until.   A.S. and O.N. til.
Tweā = two.   O.N. tweir.   A.S. twa.
Wake = watch over the dead.   O.N. vaka.
Wafs = wasp.   A.S. wōēfs.
Warsen = worse, to become worse.   A.S. versna.
Wath = a ford.   O.N. wād.
Well = to boil.   O.N. vella.
Whang = to throw, a thong.   A.S. vwang.
Whittle = a butcher's knife.   A.S. fwitel.
Wicksands = quicksands.   O.N. quicksandr.
Wife = woman, married or not.   A.S. wīf.
Winnel = a basket.   A.S. wīndel.
Winnel straw = straw for plaiting.   A.S. windel streow.
Yan = one.   A.S. ean, an.

Acknowledgements

Special thanks are extended to H.R.H. the Duke of Edinburgh and to Mrs. Cavendish, of Holker Hall. She has taken a great interest in this project and kindly allowed us to copy photographs from the family albums.

The help of the following local people is greatly appreciated:

David Braid
Jim Braid
D. Buckley
W. Benson
Desmond Burrow
Gren Burrow
Mrs. E. Butler
Derrick and Decima Cooper
J.D. Ellis
Geoff and Jacqueline Gardner
Mrs. Leah
Jack Manning
D. Proctor
Mr. Purvis
Mrs. E. Williams
Bernard Wood
and N. Wolstenholme of Morecambe, formerly of Grange-over-Sands.

Drilling in Morecambe Bay as part of a feasibility study related to a proposal to construct a water-retaining barrage. Happily, the barrage was never made.